Francis Cowley Burnand

The new history of Sandford and Merton

Francis Cowley Burnand

The new history of Sandford and Merton

ISBN/EAN: 9783337305291

Hergestellt in Europa, USA, Kanada, Australien, Japan

Cover: Foto ©ninafisch / pixelio.de

Weitere Bücher finden Sie auf **www.hansebooks.com**

THE NEW HISTORY

OF

SANDFORD AND MERTON.

Being a True Account of the Adventures of " Masters TOMMY and HARRY," with their Beloved Tutor, " Mr. BARLOW."

By F. C. BURNAND.

With Seventy-six Illustrations by

LINLEY SAMBOURNE.

SECOND EDITION.

LONDON:
BRADBURY, AGNEW, & CO., 10, BOUVERIE STREET.
1873.

LONDON:
BRADBURY, AGNEW, & CO., PRINTERS, WHITEFRIARS.

MY TWO ELDER SONS,

C. H. B. and H. C. B.

My dear

CHARLES HUBERT AND HARRY CECIL,

This book is for your instruction—negatively. Your pastors and masters will teach you what to *do*, but the New History of Sandford and Merton will, I trust, teach you what to *don't*. Beware, too, of Mr. Barlow, an immortal humbug. Avoid, in a general way, the examples set by all the characters in this volume, without exception. Be good—be virtuous, and save up your pocket-money in order to provide for your father in his old age. Thus you will ensure for yourselves many Merry Christmases and Happy New Years; and that you may enjoy a very merry holiday is the sincere wish, not only of Mr. Sambourne, who has profusely illustrated this work, but also of

    Your affectionate Father,

       F. C. BURNAND.

HALE LODGE, EDGWARE.

CONTENTS.

CHAPTER I.

SOME ANTECEDENTS OF MASTERS HENRY SANDFORD AND TOMMY MERTON; THEIR RESPECTIVE BRINGINGS-UP. CHAPTER THE FIRST BEING DEVOTED TO TOMMY . . 1

CHAPTER II.

THIS CHAPTER IS DEVOTED TO HARRY . . 6

CHAPTER III.

DEVOTED TO BOTH HARRY AND TOMMY. HERE ALSO WE ENCOUNTER FOR THE FIRST TIME MR. SANDFORD, MR. AND MRS. MERTON, AND THE RENOWNED MR. BARLOW . . 11

CHAPTER IV.

TOMMY AND HARRY AT MR. BARLOW'S. HOW THE STUDIES AND THE STORIES COMMENCED . . . 19

CHAPTER V.

STORY THE FIRST.—LEONIDAS AND THE CONCEITED PEDLAR . 24

CHAPTER VI.

WHICH CONTAINS STORY THE SECOND.—THE HERMIT AND HIS CELL 34

CONTENTS.

CHAPTER VII.

STORY THE THIRD.—THE CROCODILE AND THE PRESUMPTUOUS DENTIST 40

CHAPTER VIII.

STORY THE FOURTH (VERSES RECITED BY HARRY IN BED).—ALFONSO AND THE VOLATILE NEW-ZEALANDER . . 49

CHAPTER IX.

MASTER TOMMY AND HARRY AT WORK AND AT PLAY. THE GUNPOWDER PLOT 58

CHAPTER X.

STORY THE FIFTH.—ARSACES AND THE UNNECESSARY INFANT . 67

CHAPTER XI.

TOMMY'S ACT OF CHARITY.—HARRY'S INSTRUCTION . 83

CHAPTER XII.

STORY THE SIXTH.—THE UNCLES AND THE ANTS . 90

CHAPTER XIII.

THE BLACKBERRY FEAST AT KIND MR. MERTON'S. TOMMY'S BIRTHDAY, AND WHAT HAPPENED. THIS CONTAINS ALSO STORY THE SEVENTH.—THE HERMIT AND THE SHRIMP . 96

CHAPTER XIV.

THE SPANISH BULL-FIGHT, AS ARRANGED BY HARRY SANDFORD FOR THE AMUSEMENT OF TOMMY AND HIS YOUTHFUL COMPANIONS 108

CHAPTER XV.

DINNER OF A CONFIDENTIAL CHARACTER AT MR. MERTON'S. HARRY SANDFORD TELLS THE EIGHTH STORY.—THE HERMIT AND THE DESSERT 120

CHAPTER XVI.

OF THE SAD ILLNESS OF MR. BARLOW, AND THE KINDNESS OF HIS PUPILS. HIS GRATITUDE. THE NINTH STORY.—THE SAGE AND THE ONION 127

CHAPTER XVII.

OF HARRY AND TOMMY'S GREAT GARDENING OPERATION. MR. BARLOW TELLS THEM THE TENTH STORY . . . 144

CHAPTER XVIII.

STORY THE TENTH.—THE MAGISTRATE AND THE ELEPHANT; OR, DUTY AND PLEASURE 151

CHAPTER XIX.

SHOWING WHAT WAS THE RESULT OF MASTERS TOMMY AND HARRY'S GREAT GARDENING OPERATION . 159

CHAPTER XX.

WHAT HAPPENED TO MR. TEXTER. HARRY TELLS THE ELEVENTH STORY 16

CHAPTER XXI.

STORY THE ELEVENTH. — LEGEND OF DON DITTO AND THE DUTCHMEN ; OR, THE DEY AND THE KNIGHT . 169

CHAPTER XXII.

	PAGE
A SCHOOL-DAY OF STUDIES WITH MR. BARLOW	178

CHAPTER XXIII.

APPROACH OF HOLIDAYS. MR. BARLOW AT BRIGHTON. TOMMY'S MYSTERIOUS CONDUCT . . 193

CHAPTER XXIV.

SHOWING WHAT TOMMY MEANT BY IT. ALSO WHAT CAME OF IT, WHATEVER HE MEANT BY IT. HARRY NARRATES THE TWELFTH STORY 202

CHAPTER XXV.

STORY THE TWELFTH.—AGESILAUS AND THE ELASTIC NOBLEMAN . . 211

CHAPTER XXVI.

CONTINUATION OF THE EVENING AT FARMER SANDFORD'S 230

CHAPTER XXVII.

MASTER TOMMY MERTON'S CONTINUED RESIDENCE IN THE BOSOM OF THE SANDFORD FAMILY. MR. BARLOW'S ASTONISHING RECEPTION 236

CHAPTER XXVIII.

OF CHRISTMAS-DAY AT FARMER SANDFORD'S. HOW IT WAS SPENT. EXCITING EVENT. END 255

LIST OF ILLUSTRATIONS.

	PAGE
THE TORTURE CHAMBER .	*Frontispiece*
THE EBONY HORSE	1
THE WATER-SHED OF JAMAICA	3
"A CHEERFUL CUP OF TEA"	5
THE STUDY OF NATURAL HISTORY .	6
AND CONSEQUENT FLIGHT OF INAPPRECIATIVE INSECTS	8
ARTISTIC EMPLOYMENT OF COLOUR	10
A COCKCHAFEROUS ADVENTURE .	11
AN EVENTFUL INTERVIEW	14
FRIENDS IN COUNCIL .	16
INSTRUCTION IN HORTICULTURE	19
"THE BOWER OF BLISS"	21
"THE HEART THAT CAN FEEL FOR ANOTHER"	23
SPARTAN STEEL . .	24
THE CONCEITED PEDLAR	29
THE SAME, WITH THE CONCEIT TAKEN OUT OF HIM .	32
MELONOLOGICAL PLEASURES . . .	34

LIST OF ILLUSTRATIONS.

	PAGE
THE HERMIT AND THE INQUISITIVE BOY	37
A DECIDED SELL	38
WALNUTS AND WINE	40
THE ACHING TOOTH	42
A TRIUMPHAL MARCH	43
THE PENALTY OF PRESUMPTION	44
ALFONSO THE FORLORN	49
THE PTEREODACTYLOUS TROGOLYGDON	50
THE VAULTING VOLATILE	51
SLAP—BANG!	55
LES PETITS PATINEURS	58
INTERESTING DISCOVERY	61
"KNOWLEDGE IS POWER"	67
ASTONISHING THE NATIVES	70
"'OD RABBIT IT!"	74
AT SEA	79
"SWEETS TO THE SWEET"	83
A STILE OF MELODY	91
"THE REST WAS—SILENCE"	94
PAS DE TROIS	96
"BY THE CARD"	101
KOPROKOPOS AND THE DIGGER	103
TAKING THE BULL BY THE HORNS	108
THE CONFIDENTIAL DINNER	120

LIST OF ILLUSTRATIONS.

	PAGE
A HERMIT GETTING HIS DESSERT	125
A CLINICAL STUDY	127
THE PRACTICE OF HYDROPATHY	131
ANIMAL HEAT AND ITS SOURCES PRACTICALLY EXEMPLIFIED	138
"L'ONION FAIT LA FORCE"	142
AMATEUR GARDENING OPERATIONS	144
THE MAGISTRATE AND THE ELEPHANT	152
THE SKATING LESSON	154
A KNIGHT OF THE BATH	157
HABITANS IN SICCO	159
DOUBLE DUTCHMEN	170
DON DITTO	173
KATINKA NO WINKER	176
A STRIKING EFFECT	178
HOLIDAY ARRANGEMENTS	193
CONSOLATION FOR THE BEREAVED ONE	197
AN INEXPENSIVE SUIT	205
AGESILAUS THE VICTORIOUS	211
PLIANT DISPOSITIONS	212
A KNOTTY SUBJECT	213
THE GREEN-EYED MONSTER	215
LOVE-MAKING EXTRAORDINARY	216
THE POETRY OF MOTION	221
THE FINAL POSE	222

LIST OF ILLUSTRATIONS.

	PAGE
A SUCCESSFUL "COUP DE THEATRE" .	225
ELASTIKOS TRIUMPHANS ! .	229
TOMMY AND TODDY .	230
INGENIOUS FLY-TRICK .	234
AN EARLY-RISING MOVEMENT	236
" NO. 71, PORTRAIT OF A LADY " .	238
A TRANSFORMATION SCENE .	246
A PICTURE OF HEALTH .	247
THE FESTIVE BOAR'D .	255
A JOYFUL REUNION	264
" FAIR SHINES THE MOON TO-NIGHT "	267

THE NEW HISTORY

OF

SANDFORD AND MERTON.

CHAPTER I.

SOME ANTECEDENTS OF MASTERS HENRY SANDFORD AND TOMMY MERTON; THEIR RESPECTIVE BRINGINGS-UP. CHAPTER THE FIRST BEING DEVOTED TO TOMMY.

MISTER MERTON was a gentleman of good fortune, which he had amassed during his residence in Jamaica, where he cultivated sugar, and several other valuable things, for his own advantage.

He had only one son, Tommy Merton. He was, at this time, about ten years of age (he had been less, but the servants had received strict orders not to allude to his earlier years), and though well-disposed, irritable, affectionate, cruel, kind, and even generous in disposition, yet had he unfortunately been spoiled by too much indulgence.

As his beloved tutor, the renowned **Mr. Barlow**, used, subsequently, to say to him, "Remember, Tommy, that he who eats the sugar must also taste the cane."

While Tommy lived in Jamaica, no one was permitted, on any account, to contradict him.

Twenty negroes attended him on all occasions, one of whom invariably carried a large umbrella, and another a prodigious sunshade, in order to meet the variabilities of the climate.

If he said, during a perfect torrent of rain,

"Sambo, it's a fine day," Sambo immediately replied,

"Iss, Massa Tommy, it am, berry fine day."

"It rains," Master Tommy would then observe.

"Iss, Massa Tommy," Sambo would instantly return. "Him rain like de berry debbil."

He never went out without a palanquin, a sedan chair, an elephant, and three changes of costume, which the negroes transported from place to place.

Besides this, he was invariably dressed in silk and satins. His clothes were laced, so were his boots. His parents were so excessively fond of him that they could not restrain their tears whenever he went out for a walk, dreading lest they should never see him again, and threatening the blacks with the most awful vengeance should any sort of harm befall their Darling Treasure.

He was always helped first at dinner, and if he espied a guest served with a more delicate portion of meat than that which he had chosen for himself, a negro was at once sent to remove the choice morsel from the guest's plate and to place it before Master Tommy.

He would scramble on to the tea-table, upset the urn over his father's nankeens, throw muffins at those invited to partake of his parents' hospitality, put his foot in the butter-dish, and perform so many pranks and antics, as called forth from the delighted visitors expressions of the utmost pleasure and surprise.

No wonder that with such a bringing-up he should be beloved by his elders, and adored by his inferiors, to whom he was ever most affable and polite.

CHAPTER II.

THIS CHAPTER IS DEVOTED TO HARRY.

EAR Mr. Merton's seat in Cropshire, whither he had brought all his negro servants and his immense sugar plantations. lived a very plain honest farmer, named Sandford. This man had one son, who having been christened Harry, was usually so addressed by all who knew him. He had a good-natured countenance, the sweetest temper imaginable, and everybody loved him.

If little Harry saw a poor beggar eating his dinner by the road-side, even though it were only a crust, he would run up, and be urgent to share it with him. Nay, indeed, he would sometimes insist upon taking it all. So very kind was he, that he would go out into the fields, and climb the trees, in order to search for birds' nests. If he found them empty, he would remove them, saying, "Poor little birds! they do not know how to take care of their houses, I will keep them for them."

Often, on a similar plea, he would take away such eggs as he might find in the nests, and making a hole at either end, would blow out the yolk, observing that "by this means he had saved many a poor bird from a life of suffering and misery, from the pains of hunger and thirst, the necessities of daily labour, the cruel gun of the unskilful sportsman, or the voracious maw of the domesticated cat."

He collected live butterflies, moths, beetles, with other insects, and stuck pins through them.

So affected was he always at the sight of their fluttering when thus impaled, that he could never refrain from laughing heartily. All the animals and insects for miles round knew him,

and would get out of his way whenever he appeared in their neighbourhood, their instinct plainly telling them that any accident to *them*, would be the cause to their young friend of the utmost hilarity.

He would put thistles under the horses' tails, and have his pockets stuffed with crackers ready for distribution among the cows and pigs. If he walked in the fields, he used to select the strongest sticks from the hedges, with which he would belabour the sheep, that seeing him coming, would scamper away, leap fences and ditches, and, in some instances, would jump into the river, when they were generally drowned. Whenever so sad a fate befell any of these dumb animals, Harry would sit down and laugh as though his little sides would burst. In short he was one of the most sweet-tempered lads ever known. Farmer Jackson's bull would follow Harry wherever he went, and had often waited for him at a stile, over which he was unable to leap. Harry, observing this, would address him from the opposite side, and, while apologising for being unable to join him (as if the poor animal could indeed understand his courtesy), would wave his farewell to him with a pocket-handkerchief of a vivid red colour, which he always carried about with him for this particular purpose.

CHAPTER III.

DEVOTED TO BOTH HARRY AND TOMMY. HERE ALSO WE ENCOUNTER FOR THE FIRST TIME MR. SANDFORD, MR. AND MRS. MERTON, AND THE RENOWNED MR. BARLOW.

OMMY MERTON was once walking through a field, when he was suddenly attacked by a large cockchafer, which sprang from a tree, and coiled itself in ecstasy about his leg.

His shrieks for help soon brought Harry Sandford to his aid, who, wiping from his eyes the tears caused by an extraordinary convulsion of laughter (he had just been engaged in cutting frogs in half and plucking live ducks), sprang at Tommy, and with one blow of his stout ash-stick felled him to the earth.

" Alas ! " exclaimed Harry, on seeing Tommy fall, " that a young gentleman like this should be guilty of such cruelty to a cockchafer."

While Tommy lay insensible, Harry devoted himself to an examination of his pockets, in order to discover if the venomous insect had added theft to injury. At this moment Master Tommy's twenty black servants arrived, led by Mrs. Merton, who, on hearing from Harry how that a boa-constrictor of unusual size had attacked her son, and how that a robber, who had been hid in the long grass, had suddenly leaped up, knocked Master Tommy down, robbing him of his watch, chain, and money, " which, she would notice," he ingenuously observed, " were missing," and how he (Harry), hearing Master Tommy's cries, had rushed to the rescue, had scotched the snake, and, after a desperate encounter, had compelled the two brigands, maimed and disabled as they were, to take to their heels—when Mrs. Merton had heard all this, she gave him so sound a box on the ears as, for a few moments, almost stunned him, and taught him that the liveliest imagination, combined with descriptive faculty, are insufficient of themselves to attract an unappreciative auditory.

She now proceeded to cover her darling with kisses, and, indeed, for the next quarter of an hour, could not sufficiently exhibit her maternal solicitude, which was expending itself in the fondest caresses and the most luscious sweetmeats, when Farmer Sandford, accompanied by his son Harry, arrived on the spot.

Farmer Sandford, who was a bluff, honest man, explained in the briefest and clearest manner possible, that, not only had Master Tommy been trespassing in his fields, but that Mrs. Merton herself, and her entire retinue of dirty blacks, were also on his land, without either invitation or permission. He further accused her of violently

striking his son little Harry, who had bravely risked his own life in order to save that of Master Tommy; and he would have her to know, that as there was not one law for the sons of gentry and one for farmers' sons, he had sent down for a constable to take them all into custody, and would proceed against them at civil law for trespassing, and would have them up at the criminal bar for assault and battery, as sure as his name was Jonathan Sandford.

Mr. Merton, who had, through a powerful telescope in his observatory, witnessed the unusual excitement of the crowd in his neighbour's field, now appeared in their midst, and after sternly rebuking his wife for her injudicious conduct, tendered his apologies to the farmer, adding that he had conceived so great an admiration no less of Mr. Sandford's sterling qualities, than of Harry's courage and veracity, that nothing would satisfy him but being allowed to pay for Harry Sandford's education, conditionally upon his becoming his son's, Tommy Merton's, companion at Mr. Barlow's House.

Farmer Sandford replied that he would take an hour to deliberate upon the proposal, and if he could accept it, without compromising justice by withdrawing from the prosecution, both in the civil and criminal courts, he should feel much pleasure in so doing.

On quitting Mr. Merton, Farmer Sandford lost no time in visiting Mr. Barlow, and inquiring the

terms of tuition. Mr. Barlow replied, that for Tommy, he should charge Mister Merton, who was well able to afford it, one hundred and fifty pounds a year, exclusive of extras; but that he would take Farmer Sandford's son for fifty, which should include everything. Farmer Sandford now informed Mr. Barlow how matters stood, adding, what the future revered tutor of Masters Harry and Tommy at once comprehended, that it absolutely lay with him (Farmer Sandford), as to whether Mr. Barlow should have rich Mr. Merton's son under his care, or not.

It was finally agreed between them that the two boys should come to Mr. Barlow's; that one hundred and fifty pounds per annum should be charged for Master Merton, and one hundred, nominally, for Master Sandford, of which latter sum Mr. Barlow was to give Farmer Sandford half, payable quarterly, and was also to pay the honest farmer fifty pounds down, on the satisfactory conclusion of the agreement between Mr. Barlow and Mr. Merton, which Mr. Sandford promised to bring about.

Farmer Sandford now called upon Mr. Merton and testified his willingness to accede to the proposed arrangement, provided that the boys should commence their studies at Mr. Barlow's that very afternoon, and that Mr. Merton should there and then draw a cheque for three hundred and fifty pounds, which would represent two hundred for Master Merton's schooling and one hundred and fifty for his own son's. To this Mr. Merton at once agreed, and before three o'clock honest Farmer Sandford had cashed the cheque at the County Bank, and had paid Mr. Barlow his hundred and fifty for master Merton and his fifty for Master Sandford—minus, in both cases, three per cent Bank rate of discount for ready money, and before the County Bank closed for the day Farmer Sandford had paid in to his account one hundred pounds cash, and Mr. Barlow's bill at three months for a similar sum ; and the next morning Masters Harry Sandford and Tommy Merton commenced their educational course under Mr. Barlow's hospitable roof.

CHAPTER IV.

TOMMY AND HARRY AT MR. BARLOW'S. HOW THE STUDIES AND THE STORIES COMMENCED.

BEFORE breakfast Mr. Barlow led Harry and Tommy into his garden, and giving the former a spade, and the latter a hoe, observed,—

"Everybody who eats must assist in procuring food. Here is your bed, and here," he continued, beckoning to Tommy, "is yours.

As you make your bed so you must lie on it."

Thus saying, he withdrew to his morning meal, remembering, however, to put down in his account book, "To use of spade and hoe for Master Merton at 2s. 6d. per hour, two hours, 5s."

When Mr. Barlow had finished half a chicken, four buttered rolls, two cups of coffee, three eggs, and some marmalade on toast, he took from a cupboard a plateful of almonds and raisins, and, finding that Tommy was resting idly in the shade, while Harry was diligently working, he beckoned the latter to him, and retired into a pleasant summer-house, where he divided the almonds and raisins between Harry and himself.

At this treatment Tommy could no longer restrain his passion, and, with many oaths and protestations, declared that it was he who had been working up to within five minutes of Mr. Barlow's return to the garden, that at the invitation of Harry he had laid down to rest under a tree, while his companion had scarcely begun his labour ere Mr. Barlow stood before them.

Harry now appeared inexpressibly shocked at his young friend's perfidy, which was changed into pity on beholding him burst into a violent fit of sobbing and crying.

"What is the matter?" asked Mr. Barlow, coolly.

Poor Tommy could now scarcely reply for rage; but on perceiving Mr. Barlow unlock a small drawer and take therefrom a light and supple instrument made of apple-twigs, he would have run out of the summer-house but for Harry, who restraining him with sufficient but gentle force, said,—

"I perceive, my dear Tommy, that you are too bashful and retiring. It is I who ought to withdraw," and so saying he handed him over to Mr. Barlow, and, with the innate instinct of a true gentleman, betook himself to a convenient distance from the summer-house, where, though his ears might be pierced by the agonising shrieks of his friend, he could not do more than guess at their cause. In this sheltered nook Master Harry gave way, with a pocket-handkerchief crammed into his mouth, to all his native hilarity, and from his writhings and contortions appeared to suffer no slight pain from the necessity of controlling his laughter.

On his return to the arbour he found Mr.

Barlow sitting down, looking warm and somewhat exhausted, while Tommy was standing up and vainly struggling with such sobs, as seemed to send a tremor through his entire body.

"Your conduct, Harry and Tommy," said Mr. Barlow, "reminds me of the story of *Leonidas and the Conceited Pedlar*, which, as you have not yet heard it, I will now proceed to narrate."

CHAPTER V.

Story the First.

Leonidas and the Conceited Pedlar.

THE Spartans were a brave and hardy race. They never wanted anything that they did not get, and often got a great deal more than they wanted. Their children slept on boards and stones, and took their whack every morning. It was thus that Leonidas was brought up by his parents, who foresaw in him the future leader of their armies, and the most successful antagonist of the Persians.

Now it so chanced that when Leonidas had attained this position, a Pedlar opened his pack in the neighbourhood, and all the people, instead of attending to the wise discourses of Leonidas, surrounded the Pedlar at all hours of the day, constantly expressing their admiration of his beauty and grace, for which the Pedlar had been for some time renowned.

Leonidas now ordered him to quit the spot, that the people might return to their ordinary avocations.

The Pedlar, however, thus addressed the crowd, "My friends, am I not acknowledged to be the handsomest man ever seen? Have I not the face of Apollo, and the strength of Hercules?" Here he distributed sweetmeats among the crowd, who responded to all his questions with enthusiastic cheers. "Are not my speeches the finest speeches? Are not my jokes the best jokes ever heard? Are not my attitudes the most graceful ever seen? Yes, a hundred times, yes. Then why does Leonidas wish me to retire? because he is jealous of me, because he is afraid lest some of your money might find its way into my purse, instead of all into *his* coffers. Listen, my friends, to the ballad which I have composed, the best ballad ever written;" then striking an attitude, instead of striking a guitar, he commenced as follows :—

>   Leonidas
>   On a one-eye'd ass
>   Came riding into Athens,
>   He'd been to buy
>   A pigeon pie,
>   Likewise a pair of fat hens.

This sally was received with immense laughter and applause by the crowd, which highly relished the political allusions.

The Pedlar, finding that he had touched a chord,

now struck another attitude and continued :—

> Leonidas
> Is as monied as
> The richest king or kaiser,
> And yet 'tis true,
> 'Twixt me and you,
> That he's a thorough miser.

Here the crowd roared with delight, and the policemen, who had been indifferently peeling walnuts, looked up and smiled permissively.

The Pedlar now exerted himself to the utmost to give effect to the last verse, which ran as follows :—

> Leonidas
> Was honied as
> The little busy bee is;
> He's not a bee,
> But he's, you see,
> A hum=bug, that's what he is.

At this, the enthusiasm of the populace knew no bounds, although they literally jumped for joy, nor was their excitement allayed by the arrival of Leonidas himself, who happened to be passing that way.

He frowned as he approached the Pedlar, who, instantly changing his attitude, assumed one of such undeniable grace and dignity, as was calculated to affect the beholders above anything they had ever seen before.

"Are you aware—" Leonidas commenced.

"No, Leonidas," replied the Conceited Pedlar, interrupting him; "I am not *a ware*, because I am a pedlar. Where are you now?"

"You know what I mean," said Leonidas, who was in no humour for trivial jesting.

"You are indeed polite," responded the Pedlar, altering his position, "to credit me with greater knowledge than that possessed by yourself." Here he bowed to the ground, threw his legs up in the air, walked on his hands, turned two somersaults, and then alighting on his feet in a new attitude, observed, "Here we are again!"

"I believe," said Leonidas, "that you do not know what wares are. Your wares are your goods."

"Nay," quoth the Pedlar, "my wares are more than my goods, for they are my bests, and the best that money can procure."

Leonidas strode on, and was soon lost to view. That night, when the Conceited Pedlar was supposed to be sleeping, Leonidas peered in through a hole in the canvas, and there saw the pedlar hard at work, alternately learning jests and repartees by heart from a goodly volume, and copying attitudes, from pictures, before a large mirror. Lighting a drug, Leonidas contrived so that its narcotic fumes should reach the Conceited Pedlar's nose, who thereupon gradually fell asleep. Leonidas now entering, and taking possession of the book and the pictures, silently withdrew.

The next day the Pedlar in vain attempted to arrest the attention of his audience; but as he struck no new attitudes, and made no jokes which they had not already heard, their patience was soon exhausted.

In order to save him from the justly incensed mob, the civil guards brought him before Leonidas, who immediately commanded him to submit himself to the hands of his own skilled surgeons, who, being perfectly acquainted with the anatomy of the human frame, would know exactly where to make the incision in order to remove the immense amount of conceit which was in him.

His cries and supplications were all in vain. "Give us," exclaimed Leonidas, before the whole tribunal, "one new and original jest *which I shall not be able to find in this book.* Strike one new and original attitude *which I do not see in these pictures,* and your sentence shall be mitigated."

The Conceited Pedlar uttered a piercing shriek, and fell back into the arms of the attendants.

* * * * *

Three days afterwards Leonidas exhibited to the Spartans a man whose head hung down upon his breast, whose limbs were limp and helpless, and whose entire demeanour presented such a picture of dejection as the people had never seen equalled.

"This," said Leonidas, "is the Pedlar, with *the Conceit taken out of him.*"

A yell of derision broke from the multitude. Leonidas produced the book and the pictures, and explained to the crowd the use to which the Pedlar had hitherto put them.

Then he returned them to the Pedlar, who, to the surprise of all, suddenly appeared re-animated with a new vigour. In less time than it takes to relate, he had opened the portfolio of pictures, and collecting all his strength for one final spring, *he threw himself into an attitude, and disappeared for ever.*

"What has become of him?" inquired the former admirers of the Conceited Pedlar, of Leonidas.

Leonidas significantly placed his dexter finger of his dexter hand perpendicularly against his nose, with such mathematical precision as to bisect that organ at a given point, so as to form with the two sides meeting it an equilateral triangle, of which the tip of the nose was the third angle. He said nothing, but he smiled again several times to himself during the remainder of his life.

CHAPTER VI.

WHICH CONTAINS STORY THE SECOND.

THE following morning Mr. Barlow, who, since the arrival of his two pupils, had dismissed his gardener, sent them into his garden to turn up the earth in order to prepare it for his potatoes, beans, and celery, of all which vegetables he was an ardent consumer.

When the two boys had got well out of sound and sight of their tutor's house, Harry, seating himself under a tree, commenced eating an apple which he had brought with him, and which his friend Tommy proposed should be shared by them in two equal portions.

Harry Sandford now playfully observed that he had considered Tommy too much of a gentleman to eat so vulgar a fruit as an apple, at which rebuke poor Tommy hung down his head and blushed so deeply that Harry, who was far from being of a niggardly disposition, honestly wished that he had another apple which he did not want himself, as in that case he vowed he would have immediately bestowed it upon his friend, unless he had kept it by him until he should require it more than he did at the present moment. Tommy was so deeply touched by this conduct that, laying down his hoe, he insisted upon telling his companion the story of *The Hermit and the Cell*, " which," he said, " as you have not yet heard it, I will proceed to narrate."

Story the Second.

The Hermit and his Cell.

A RUDE little boy on his daily walk to school used often to meet a bare-footed Hermit. The Hermit was unable to stay the boy and answer such of his questions as "How's your mother?" "How are you to-morrow?" "Who's your hatter?" "How's your poor feet?" and "Where's your cell?"

One morning, however, the lad ran right against the bare-footed Hermit, who, taking him by the collar, asked wherefore he had hitherto avoided him.

"Please, sir, don't!" cried the little boy

The Hermit spake kindly to him, and informed him first of all that his mother, for aught he knew, was well; secondly, that one day being to him very like another, or more so, he was therefore as healthy to-morrow as yesterday or the day afterwards; thirdly, that as he did not wear hats it was impossible to give him the address of his hatter; and fourthly, that his feet needed no pity, having never been used to boots. "And as to

where my cell is," continued the holy man in conclusion, "with that you shall soon become acquainted. You shall visit me," said he, kindly, "and you will see that I have a surprise in store for you. I inhabit a hut which is rude, but I myself am invariably polite. Do you like jam?"

The little boy replied that he was rapturously attached to preserve.

"Come, then," said the Hermit, "after school hours."

The lad, accordingly, ran out into the desert, and saw the hut standing under a palm-tree.

"Come in," said the Hermit's voice, apparently from within.

The little boy rushed eagerly towards the door, which was standing ajar, and pulled it open; when lo! down came upon his head a huge jam-pot

entirely filled with the dirtiest water from a stagnant pond. For a few minutes the boy lay as one stunned, while the Hermit, who had been hitherto concealed behind a bush, came out and belaboured him soundly.

The boy arose, but before he could hurry off, the Hermit said to him,—

"You came greedily expecting jam. This, my dear child, is

The Hermit's Sell."

CHAPTER VII.

Story the Third.

The Crocodile and the Presumptuous Dentist.

"WHAT, sir, is a crocodile?" inquired Tommy one day of Mr. Barlow.

Mr. Barlow, who was at that moment engaged in steeping walnuts, which he had himself deprived of their cuticle, in a wine-glassful of sherry, paused for a moment and then replied,—

"The crocodile, my dear Tommy, is a cruel

creature that lives almost entirely on hardboiled eggs."

"That is indeed remarkable," observed Harry.

"And when there are no eggs?" asked Tommy.

"Then, my dear Tommy," answered Mr. Barlow, "it lives upon the shore. It takes its food hot."

Mr. Barlow was now about to resume his occupation with the walnuts, when Harry eagerly inquired,—

"But pray, sir, does it never devour men?"

Mr. Barlow now turned towards Harry, while Tommy, who was on the opposite side of the table, drew his chair nearer to the walnuts. Their beloved tutor, without noticing this movement of Master Tommy's, thus commenced,—

"The Crocodile, as I have said, liking its food hot, will never devour a man as long as he is sufficiently cool. This reminds me of the story of *The Crocodile and the Presumptuous Dentist*, which, as you have neither of you heard it, I will now proceed to narrate. A young Dentist was once lying asleep by the side of a river, when he was aroused by a prodigious sobbing, and on raising his eyes to the spot whence these lugubrious sounds proceeded, he was astonished at perceiving an enormous Crocodile coming towards him with open mouth, and

from time to time pointing, as well as it could, with its fore paw to a huge tooth which lay far back in its upper jaw. The Dentist, divining the cause of the creature's tears, forthwith produced his instruments, and, after a careful scrutiny, he dexterously extracted the molar, which had been the occasion to the Crocodile of so much agony. After this nothing would serve the grateful animal's turn but that the Dentist should ride on his back everywhere, and in this way the courageous young man travelled over Egypt without incurring the slightest expense. Subsequently the Dentist tried to induce the Crocodile to have a set of false teeth, when the

honest animal, suspecting some treachery, ate him. Thus you see," said Mr. Barlow, in conclusion, "even gratitude cannot tolerate presumption."

Mr. Barlow, by this time, bethought him of his walnuts, which should have been well soaked in the sherry, and would have afforded him considerable refreshment. Instead of which he only saw by his side an empty glass, and turning to make further inquiry of Master Tommy, he found, to his astonishment, that his young pupil had disappeared.

"I did not like, sir," said Harry, "to interrupt your discourse, or had I done so it would have been to inform you, sir, that while you were talking, Master Tommy was engaged in rapidly devouring those nuts which you had, with such admirable care and forethought, put aside for your own consumption."

"You shall not," observed Mr. Barlow, "lose by your politeness, and as I perceive that our young friend has made his escape by the window—"

"I," interrupted Master Harry readily, "while you are closing it, will retire by the door." So saying, and ere Mr. Barlow, whose foot had caught in the corner of the drugget, could recover from the effect of suddenly coming in contact with the sharp edge of the dining-table, Harry ran out, and finding Tommy alone in a secluded part of the garden, insisted upon receiving his portion of the nuts, which Tommy had in dumb show promised him.

Tommy now vowed and protested, on his word of honour as a gentleman, that his companion had completely misunderstood the purport of the signs, which, he admitted, he had made behind their revered tutor's back.

Master Harry proceeded at once to give him so severe a chastisement that Master Tommy offered him all that remained of his week's pocket-money if he would desist, which Harry, who was a boy of really generous spirit, consented, on this understanding, to do.

The same night, after they were in bed, Mr. Barlow, carrying the rod, and accompanied by the butler, entered their room.

* * * * *

In addition Master Tommy had to take a strong dose of the most nauseous medicine possible. The butler before retiring had brought into the apartment a small table on which were spread out a variety of luscious fruits, with a bottle of golden sherry and a plate of picked walnuts.

"You are fond of these?" observed Mr. Barlow, seating himself and commencing the repast; "you shall see me eat them. But as I told you a story while Master Tommy ate my walnuts, you shall now, Master Harry, tell *me* a story while Master Tommy, who is not likely to sleep for some time to come, shall look on and listen. Tell me then, Harry, does not our present position remind you of anything that you have either heard or read?"

"Indeed, sir," replied Harry, with some emotion, "it does. It recalls the tale of *Alfonso and the Volatile New Zealander*, which——"

"As we have never heard——" observed Mr. Barlow, peeling an orange.

"I will now proceed to narrate," said Master Harry, turning his pillow cool side uppermost, and sitting on it in bed.

"Once upon a time," said Harry, "when the animals which we now call pigs——"

"Stop, if you please, Harry," said Mr. Barlow, sucking his third walnut, "you will oblige me by repeating this tale in verse."

"But, sir," said Master Harry, "I am unable to remember——"

"Nay, my dear Harry," returned Mr. Barlow, "if that be the case, I must see what the magic of the divining rod may——"

"Do not rise, sir, on my account," interrupted Harry, with the utmost consideration, "I will at once comply with your request."

CHAPTER VIII.

Story the Fourth.

VERSES RECITED BY HARRY IN BED.

Alfonso and the Volatile New Zealander.

Alfonso once had lost his way,
He roamed o'er mountain, sea, and bay,
By coach, by ship, by horse, by shay.

For two long years in vain he tried
To hear some tidings of his bride,
For two more years he tried in vain,
And then began to try again.
For where she'd gone they did not know,
But nobody dared tell him so.

He landed on a foreign shore,
He heard the lions howl and roar,
He heard the Trogolygdon's* note,

* "*A Ptercodactylous animal,*" explained *Mr. Barlow*, subsc-

And straightway gat him to his boat.

He saw, upon the mountain top,
A man whose head was like a mop,

He had two spindle-shankian legs,
And two large eyes as big as eggs.

His mouth was flat, his ears were brown,

quently, " by which is meant an animal of the Poet's creation, something between a Stereoscope and a Dactyl."

His nose was sort of upside down,
His teeth were as the teeth of shark,
And he was soaring like a lark.

He had a bright and polished chin,
His arms were long, his hands were thin ;
He perched upon the mountain edge,
Then 'lighted on a rocky ledge.
And he was singing all the while,
" I'm Volatile ! I'm Volatile ! "

He bounded lightly o'er the plain,
Sprung up, then darted down again,
And then he skimmed the little waves.
" Dear me, how strangely he behaves ! "
Thus said Alfonso as he stared,
For information scarce he dared
    To ask this Being quaint.
At last he shouted, " How d'ye do ? "
The man replied, " What's that to you ? "
Alfonso said, " Are you a Jew ? "
    He answered, " No, I ain't."

"My dress is made of coloured rags,
I wear no—what are known as 'bags,'—
　　I only have a kilt.
And I am—not a Hielander—
A Volatile New Zealander,
　　Remarkably well built."

"Oh, stay a bit," Alfonso said,
"And on a pillow rest your head!"
The man replied, "I don't like bed,
　　I'm Volatile!"

"I'll give you luncheon, if you'll stop,"
Alfonso cried, "a pint and chop,
If you'll one minute cease to hop,
　　Young Volatile!"

Alfonso spread his luncheon out,
Two chops, imperial pint of stout,
And one of port—he feared not gout—
　　And said, "Sir, may I tempt you?"

Adding, " Don't dance about, because
You'll never win from me applause.
New Zealander, no sort of laws
    From hunger can exempt you."

" I am so Volatile," said he.
Alfonso says, " Yes, that may be ;
But don't go splashing in the sea,
    As thus, you see, you wet me.
Could I exhibit him," he thought,
" He'd be a fortune if once caught ;
Come down," he cried, " and try some port."
    " I wish that you may get me ! "

He cried, " I know your little game,
Thankye for nothing, all the same,
The Volatile is still my name,
    Than Wieland I am Wielander ;
Touch me can neither Payne nor Vokes,
Nor all your Bounding Brother Folks,
    The Volatile New Zealander ! "

He bounded towards the rising sun :
Alfonso took a loaded gun.

He bounded towards the crimson rock :
Alfonso got the gun full cock.

Now right, now left, now left, now right,
Alfonso couldn't fix his sight:
All day until the light grew dim
The Volatile made game of him;
And sometimes in the wave he'd splash,
Then on the mountain-top he'd dash.

A tree Alfonso had his eyes on,
He sprang off that to the horizon;
Alfonso said, " He's out of range,
I wish he'd his position change.
Now I will shoot him while he flits!"
Bang! and the gun went all to bits.

It blew the row-boat into shivers,
Some pieces fell in far-off rivers;
And as he sank Alfonso cried,
" I never now shall find my bride."

And all the time his voice was sounding,
The Volatile still went on bounding;
Until upon the sand, at length,
He summoned all his mighty strength,

He took a most gigantic run,
Then jumped—and cleared the Setting Sun.

And where he's gone there's none can say ;
But this is known—he's gone away,
Being too Volatile to stay.

And where Alfonso's bride may be
Is nothing much to you or me ;
And as Alfonso couldn't swim,
It matters not one bit to him.
What after did to her befall
Is of no consequence at all.

At the conclusion of the ballad, Mr. Barlow, taking the sugar with him, and leaving only some orange-peel and walnut-shells on the table, quitted the apartment, and Harry, after waking Tommy with a wet sponge from the sound sleep into which he had fallen, soon fell into a delicious slumber, and an hour afterwards both boys were fast asleep.

CHAPTER IX.

MASTER TOMMY AND HARRY AT WORK AND AT PLAY.
THE GUNPOWDER PLOT.

HE little boys were now indeed enjoying themselves. In the early morning they went out skating (an amusement which Mr. Barlow had strictly forbidden them to indulge in), and towards the latter end of the month nothing gave them greater pleasure than to hire guns and go out shooting, which Mr. Barlow had desired them on no account to think of doing. As they now commenced to understand that no pleasure brings with it such contentment and true happiness as that which has been prohibited by competent authority, so they had already begun to experience those joys which invariably accompany such pursuits as had not received the approbation of their beloved tutor. For several hours during the day they were engaged in digging what they said were the foundations of a new house for Mr. Barlow, their real design being, under cover of such apparently useful industry, to make a secret communication with the cellars of their beloved tutor's house. To this they had been incited by the perusal of such tales as *The Boy Guy Fawkes, The Little Highwayman, Master Henry and his Brigands*, and other delightful publications of a similar character, which, since Tommy had acquired the art of reading with facility, had been within reach of their purses, and had afforded them no small amount of gratification and healthy excitement.

Mr. Merton, who was a very wealthy man, had been easily prevailed upon to send his son money, which Harry laid out for both of them in gunpowder, crackers, pistols, and the most explosive fireworks. These they kept secreted in barrels, with a view to placing them, on the first opportunity, in the cellars under Mr. Barlow's house.

Their elaborate design would, doubtless, have met with a success beyond their most sanguine expectations, had not Tommy been induced by his vanity to give a Pyrotechnical Display on, what he termed, the laying of the first stone of the Foundations. The fireworks let off upon this occasion were indeed well worthy of the event they were intended to commemorate, and set fire to two hayricks in a neighbouring field, at the same time that the stick from a rocket passed through the thatched roof of Farmer Johnson's stable; the fires being in both cases extinguished with no slight difficulty.

Farmer Sandford being called in to estimate the loss, it soon appeared that the damage was of such magnitude as could only be covered by a large cheque out of Mr. Merton's book, which would save Master Tommy from being charged with incendiarism before the nearest Justice of the Peace.

Mr. Barlow now instituted a strict search, and was pleased beyond measure at finding a train of

gunpowder so laid as to pass through a hole in the basement of his own residence, the consequences of which would, at an instant's notice, probably prove fatal to the house itself and its inhabitants.

On being questioned, Harry, who was of a noble disposition, at once replied that as there was nothing to conceal, he would immediately tell the whole truth, which, indeed, he said, it gave him great pain to say, would show that Master Tommy was solely to blame in this affair. Master Merton had been studying the science of engineering, and their conversation had been turned upon blasting experiments, which, Harry admitted, had for both of them considerable attraction. That Master Tommy had insisted upon trying its effect on their beloved tutor, " a proposition," added Harry, " against which my whole soul revolted." That, in fact, Master Merton had done it all, and had compelled him to silence with fearful oaths and threats, which was the ordinary method for preserving inviolable secresy used by the Secret Political Society of which he was afraid Master Tommy was a distinguished member, if not indeed a chief.

Having received this astounding intelligence, Master Harry Sandford was requested to withdraw into a private apartment, during the separate examination of Master Merton. Tommy, who had that very morning received a handsome sum of money from his generous father, advanced towards Mr. Barlow, and looked at him as though he had some weighty matter to disclose, but was unable to give it utterance. Mr. Barlow, therefore, turned towards him with the utmost kindness, and, taking him tenderly by the hand, was much pleased to find in it three sovereigns, two half crowns, and a shilling, " which," said Tommy, almost crying, " I am afraid will not repay you for all the trouble and annoyance that I have occasioned you."

Mr. Barlow. " When you are so sensible as you have now shown yourself, my little friend, then you deserve everybody's friendship and esteem. Few people are so perfect,"—here Mr. Barlow slightly blushed on hearing Harry's voice through the keyhole, saying, " hear, hear ! "—" few people are so perfect as not to err sometimes" ("*No, No!*" from Harry in the next room). "But I am as happy to accept the evidence of your sorrow, as I shall be to receive the account of your error."

Tommy. "Indeed, sir, I am rejoiced to hear you say so. You must know then, sir," here he sunk his voice to a whisper, "that everything I do is entirely owing to Harry Sandford's fault, in whose company I am likely to become a worse boy than ever I was before." Tommy now raised his tone and continued loudly, "Yet, sir, so fond and attached am I to young Harry, and so intimately associated am I with him in all our amusements and employments, that I readily own, that if you, sir," here once more he resumed the lower key, "only punish Harry *sufficiently*, I shall indeed feel most acutely for him, and suffer all those agonies of remorse of which the occasion permits."

Mr. Barlow commended Tommy very much for dispositions so full of kindliness and goodness, and taking up his apple-twig rod, gave him a sound flogging, which was only interrupted by a hearty laugh that reached them through the keyhole, whereupon Mr. Barlow, taking his leave of Master Tommy, went to communicate with Master Sandford.

"You have," observed Mr. Barlow to him on entering, "the noblest mind that ever adorned a human being, and I shall not be happy until I have been able to make your body equal to it in all respects."

So saying he proceeded to mark the day, as he said, in unmistakable red letters.

"Your conduct," said Mr. Barlow, when in the evening of the same day they were all sitting down cheerfully to their evening meal, "your conduct reminds me of the story of *Arsaces and the Unnecessary Infant*, which as you have neither of you heard it——"

"I fancy, sir," said Harry, "that I have."

"Then," resumed Mr. Barlow, "you can put down the bread and jam which you have just spread for yourself, and narrate the story to myself and Master Tommy, who, being less instructed in the tale, will proceed with our repast."

Master Harry now begged to be excused, especially as he observed Tommy eyeing his slice of bread and jam; but as his tutor would take no denial, he contented himself with giving Tommy so smart an application under the table, as, occasioning Tommy to cry out suddenly, called forth a reproof from Mr. Barlow for interrupting his friend with such a noise, and before Tommy had time to explain, Harry had commenced the story which will be found in the following chapter.

CHAPTER X.

Story the Fifth.

Arsaces and the Unnecessary Infant.

HE venerable Arsaces once passed several months among the Arabians, whose simplicity of life and innocence of manners greatly delighted him. They arose at three in the afternoon, and before their evening meal they had often left whole villages in flames, and taken captive several barbarians, whose wives and helpless children they had previously massacred with all the gentleness of which they were capable. Arsaces, who had lived in the principal cities of the world only to know their emptiness, had determined upon retiring to some sequestered spot, in order to devote himself to the study of various feats of legerdemain with cards and half-crowns, "the knowledge of which," said this astute old man to himself, "is undoubted power."

Here dwelling peacefully in the Arab encampments, safe from the rapacity of greed, the vindictiveness of creditors, and from the inquisitive visits of messengers from the Court, Arsaces began to realise the sweets of true enjoyment. He married a virtuous young woman, and in her society experienced a far less degree of tranquillity than generally falls to the lot of man. She starved the cattle, killed the sheep and goats, while Arsaces confined himself to such speculations as were not only sublime and consolatory to the human heart, but afforded promise of a bright and happy future. He wandered among the neighbouring mountains, and in some tranquil nook amid the awful roar of the stupendous cataract, or in secluded spots where the violence of storms had borne away the rocks, he would produce a pack of cards and gradually master the mysterious doctrine of chances, while in the waterfall he would see his own actions clearly mirrored, and would only be satisfied with himself as having attained perfection in any one instance when he was unable to detect his own method of operating reflected in the pure and limpid stream before him. His favourite employment was to stray among the simple peasants whom he would find tending their flocks, reposing after their mid-day meal, or resting from the labours of the day. With these he was ever gentle and affable, and never let an opportunity escape him of asking them to choose a card, when he would astonish them by producing the one which they had chosen, or of which perhaps they had only thought.

Nor was his affability confined to these instances alone, for on the days when the artless peasants were returning with their week's wages in their wallets, he would meet them, and ask them if they would not wager him so much that a certain

small pea, which he had carefully dried for the purpose, was, or was not, underneath a certain thimble, three of which he invariably kept about him, "as," he observed, "an agriculturist ought to have about him the implements, for *sewing*." By thus rendering services useful to his fellow-creatures, who never could either rightly guess where the pea was hidden, nor plumb the mystery of the three-card trick, he received the purest reward which can attend the increase of knowledge, the consciousness of always doing, and of never being done in return.

One only child was the fruit of the union of Arsaces with the mother of the infant Sellani, for that was the name which his offspring was destined to bear.

But alas, such a life was too unchequered to last. The wife of Arsaces one morning quitted his roof, (she was generally on the roof, because in Eastern countries it is cooler than indoors) leaving him the sole charge of the child Sellani.

On the baby's breast was pinned this paper written in a trembling hand :—

"*I can put up with you no longer. I am now putting up without you at an Inn. I pity and forgive you. The child is not mine, because I was myself changed at nurse, and you have married my sister who is little aware of the cruel treatment I have experienced. I belong to a family which was always being changed at birth, and my great grandfather, who is alive and well now, is not yet quite himself. I know how you do the three-card trick and the little pea. With this knowledge you are in my power. In remembrance of you as you once were, and as some fond souvenirs of yourself, I have taken with me everything of value that I could lay hands upon about the place. Tell the child to think of her mother as if she was her aunt's first cousin, but do not change her again, as there is no knowing what she may turn out. I have met an old servant of our family who says she notices the alteration in my features which she attributes entirely to my having been changed for somebody else—perhaps more than once.*

" *Farewell.*"

Arsaces was seized with inexpressible distress on finding himself thus bereaved. He had now to endure a bitter persecution from the authorities, who, in the first week of his enforced widowhood, fined him three times for keeping a child without a licence.

This embittered the proud spirit of Arsaces, who, leaving the infant at the door of Migrashus the chief magistrate, quitted the place for ever.

Arsaces now recommenced life in the large cities. His assiduous duties were at last about to find their recompense. The marvellous problem involved in the Three Thimbles, and the Little Pea, no less than in that of the Three Cards, absorbed the attention of the greatest philosophers and men of science of that time, and divided the kingdom into parties, until at length political partizanship being introduced on either side, the reigning Dynasty was upset, the sole representative of a long line of kings was forced to fly the country, of which the people, rising as one man, offered the crown to the popular Arsaces, on the sole condition that he should once more show them how he could place an orange under a cover, and, on subsequently lifting it up, discover a rabbit in its place.

The orange was secreted, and Arsaces, amidst profound silence pledged himself to the result.

He removed the cover, and resting under it was no rabbit, but an Infant, which Arsaces at once recognised as his own.

Stupefied at the sight, he was about to appeal to the spectators, when the child, standing upright on the table, addressed the populace with so much tact and energy, that the unstable crowd, crying,

"Arsaces to the gallows! Arsaces to the block! Arsaces to the stake!" tore up the benches and demanded their money back. Suddenly the lights were extinguished, and in the darkness, which Arsaces had cunningly foreseen would ensue from this device, he made his escape, but this time with the Infant on his back, whom he was now convinced would be either the burden or the joy of his chequered career.

As he was crossing the Euphrates one dark night——

"Pray stop," said Mr. Barlow, " I wish to ask Tommy a question. Why is it dark at night?"

Tommy considered for a moment and then answered,—

" Because, sir, the moon shines."

Mr. Barlow threw the milk-jug at him, and Harry forthwith proceeded with his narrative.

As he was crossing the Euphrates, one dark night, the boat upset, and when Arsaces had reached in safety the opposite bank, the Infant was nowhere to be found.

Arsaces now worked with redoubled zeal and perseverance, and was not long before he had acquired so excellent a reputation in Sparta as to insure him engagements for at least four nights in the week at private parties, while he occasionally managed to delight and astonish crowded audiences in the theatre, when other performances were not going on.

On one of these occasions a noble lady was so struck no less by the grace of his bearing than by his highly entertaining qualities, that, carried away by her curiosity to learn the secret of the Three Thimbles, she offered him her hand and fortune, which was considerable.

Arsaces could not withstand the importunities of the fair Persian—for she was a native of that country—and at length agreed to render her happy by naming the day for their nuptials, when he would also, he said, inform her how the Three Thimbles were done.

When the friends of the bride were assembled, and the ceremony was about to commence, a veiled woman entered bearing a basket, which she offered to the Persian lady. Before Arsaces could interfere, Sellani—for it was she—sat up in her *berceau*, and not only declared herself to be his child, but introduced the veiled lady as his wife.

Arsaces, obliged to fly the country, now became a wanderer over the earth. Wherever he went, whenever he attempted to puzzle the people with his Thimbles and Three Cards, the Infant was sure to be on the spot to explain how they were done.

In the meantime the Persians had taken up arms to resent the affront offered to their countrywoman, and the Spartans, ever eager for battle, at once commenced hostilities. Arsaces told the latter that victory was on the cards. The engagement began, and Arsaces was seen conspicuous in every part of the field encouraging his companions to charge. Five times he was observed running with all his might towards, as he said, the place where he supposed the enemy to be thickest. Brought back on every occasion by his brave companions, he at last fell, gloriously, into the hands of the enemy.

Heroically refusing to accept his life on any terms short of showing his countrymen's plan of battle to their foes, he was at once, on his offer being accepted, brought before the general.

Producing from his satchel his Three Thimbles, which he now named the tents of the enemy, he was proceeding to interest the chiefs of the army, when a voice from the interior of the tent exclaimed, "Beware!"

Arsaces recognised the tone, it was that of the neglected Infant. Rushing headlong once more into the midst of the affray, Arsaces was seen no more.

*   *   *   *

Next morning a dishonest mariner, who ought *not* to have been loitering on the shore at eleven o'clock on the previous night, but had been doing so, informed a young man, who did not happen to be much interested in the matter, that he had seen three figures sailing out to sea in a small boat. Two, a man and a woman, were seated in the prow, the one explaining to the other something with what appeared to be pieces of cardboard, while in the stern sat what seemed to be a prodigiously fine baby, steering.

It was doubtless Arsaces and his craft. This supposition is rendered the more probable by the fact that the vessel was thimble-rigged.

Tommy expressed himself vastly delighted with the story, to which he had listened with such attention during tea-time as to have taken no account of the many slices of bread and jam which he had consumed, although they had been, in reality, prepared for his friend Harry, who now found himself reduced to a single round of dry bread.

"Think, however," said Mr. Barlow, reverentially, "how many poor starving people there are to whom this would be a luxury. Tommy, lock up the jam-pot and give me the key."

Tommy obeyed, and, on Mr. Barlow quitting the room, was about to follow him, when Harry whispered,—

"Poor people be blowed! Look here, I'll punch your head afterwards."

"We will now," said Mr. Barlow, returning,

"go out into the garden and look at the stars."

So saying, he handed them their telescopes, and having seen them safely into the garden, he carefully shut and locked the house-doors and retired to bed, where, with a smile upon his lips betokening much inward enjoyment, he soon fell into a sound sleep, from which he was only aroused half-an-hour afterwards by the cry of fire, and, on putting his head out of window, he received full in his face the contents of the garden-engine, which Harry and Tommy were, with great presence of mind, energetically pumping.

The alarm, however, proving to be false, Mr. Barlow thanked them in a neat speech from his bedroom window, and begged them to enter the house by the back door, which was now unlocked. But Tommy, however, perceiving, through a crack, the burly figure of the butler secreted behind it, allowed Harry to adopt this mode of entrance, when he was immediately seized by the faithful domestic, while he himself ascended by a ladder to his bedroom, the door and window of which he secured before resting for the night, and no entreaties, either of his young companion or the butler, could arouse him from the sudden deep slumber into which, after the fatigues of the day, he had fallen.

So Harry, who had a liking for hardships, spent the night in the spare room, which Mr. Barlow had recently furnished very handsomely, intending it for the reception of such of his pupils' relations as might honour him with their presence.

Harry was, however, too tired to examine the furniture that night. But putting off his carpentering experiments for the present, he too was soon as fast asleep as the other inmates of the house.

CHAPTER XI.

TOMMY'S ACT OF CHARITY.—HARRY'S INSTRUCTION.

ONE morning Tommy said to Harry,—

"I have received from my father some money for a starving family in the village, and I am going to buy them something to eat."

Harry applauded his friend's generous resolution, and promised to conduct him to the sweet shop, where he could lay out the sum, which his father had sent him for this charitable purpose, to his heart's content.

The two boys now set out for Mrs. Brown's, where Tommy bought five shillings' worth of brandy-balls, lollipops, hardbake, almond rock, and toffy.

These were made up into a parcel, which Harry kindly offered to carry for him.

Tommy, however, declined his friend's proposal, whereupon Harry observed that he had thought Tommy too much of a fine gentleman to carry such a load himself.

To this Tommy only replied, that if he found it overburdening his strength, he could easily relieve it of some of its contents.

Harry. Would it not be better if we spent one penny in bread for these poor people, and ate these good things ourselves?

Tommy. I protest that you are welcome to buy

a loaf for them if you will, and, for my part, I am so far of your opinion, that I have already diminished the weight of the parcel by three brandy-balls.

Harry. That is indeed clever; and now, my dear Tommy, as you possess the money, you can run on to the baker's, while I remain here with the bag.

Tommy. I would willingly agree to your plan, if it were not for giving you so much trouble, which I am by this time well able to undertake myself. So do you rest here, while I go to the baker's for the bread, and as there is no necessity for leaving the sweets with you, I will take them with me.

Harry. Stay, Master Tommy, do you know of what bread is made?

Tommy. No, certainly; and I own that I have no curiosity on the subject.

Harry. Then I will tell you. Before you put that next piece of toffy in your mouth, let me inform you that bread is made of wheat resembling the oats which you have sometimes given to Mr. Barlow's horse. Would you like to feed on what Mr. Barlow's horse does?

Tommy. That indeed, Harry, would go against the grain.

Harry. True; but do you know how the bread comes, then?

Tommy. Why they send the baker's boy with it every morning. Did you never see him?

Harry. Yes, I have; but be good enough to answer my question; where do they send the oats to, in order to make them into bread?

Tommy. To Jericho, perhaps.

Harry. No, Tommy, not to Jericho, but to be ground.

Tommy. How can it be ground if it is bread?

Harry. Before it is bread it has to be ground in a mill.

Tommy. And what, pray, is a mill?

Harry (*taking off his jacket*). A mill is something, which, as you are not already acquainted with it, I will proceed to show you. And in order that no part of the process may be incomplete, I will begin by giving you a sound thrashing.

Tommy now earnestly begged him to accept the bag for himself, in which more than half the sweetmeats yet remained untouched. But Harry, with a look of more contempt than he had ever been seen to assume before, accepted the present, and, putting on his jacket, walked away accompanied by his companion.

When Harry had finished the contents of the parcel, he inquired where the starving family dwelt in whom Tommy had appeared so deeply interested.

At this question poor Tommy blushed and hung down his head. Harry now repeated his question, and requested an instant answer unless he wished him to go at once to their revered tutor, in order to confide to Mr. Barlow his suspicions concerning his young friend's conduct.

"Harry," answered Tommy, a little confused, "I will not deceive you. Deception, I have always heard, is the better part of valour. My father, relying entirely upon the statements in my letter, which were framed in the most poetic fashion, and coloured with all the fervent ardour of a glowing imagination, sent me the money that has provided us with the sweetmeats, of which, I may now remind you, you have eaten by far the greater portion."

"I understand," said Harry, rising; "but remember that I have not yet taught you how bread is made."

Tommy assured his companion that he would never again afford him the opportunity of resuming his instruction, and that, for his part, he vowed and protested, that, neither to their tutor, nor to any other person, would he mention one single word of what he had confided to him.

It being now the hour for their early dinner, they walked leisurely home, without meeting with any further adventure.

When their frugal repast was concluded, Tommy and Harry were for lying at full length on the grass, and taking what the honest Italian people are in the habit of calling a *siesta*.

"Your conduct," said Mr. Barlow, addressing his beloved pupils, "reminds me of the story of *The Uncles and the Ants*, which as neither of you have heard it, I will now proceed to narrate."

Thus saying Mr. Barlow produced his accordion, on which he was more than a proficient, and requesting Tommy to hold the music while Harry should turn over the leaves, he thus commenced:

CHAPTER XII.

Story the Sixth.

The Uncles and the Ants.

Two Uncles sat upon a stile
    One fine autumnal day,
The elder one allowed a smile
    Upon his face to play;
The younger Uncle said, " May I,
My relative, inquire why
    You are so very gay?"

The elder Uncle took and played
    A tune upon his fife,
And then, " I smile because," he said,
    " I'm here without my wife."

The younger one produced a pie,
As he responded, " So am I.
  Oblige me with a knife."

The elder said, " If you can spare
  Of toothsome pie a slice,
My ginger-beer with you I'll share,
  You'll find it very nice."
The younger said, " Well, just one drop
Of effervescent ginger-pop,
  I'll take by your advice."

They took their pie and gingerade,
    And sat upon the ground,
And they ingeniously made
    A table of a mound.
" This pie, indeed, is first-rate paste."
" This ginger-beer is to my taste."
    And then they smiled all round.

Then as the pop began to flow,
    Its ginger sought their brain,
They loudly chanted, " We won't go
    Till morning home again."
And quoth the elder with a leer,
" I rather think this ginger-beer
    Is stronger than champagne."

They told their daring deeds of youth
    In spite of angry pa's,
Alas! they spoke with little truth
    Of their respective ma's.

They spoke of hammering and nails,
Of sparrows and of salted tails,
   While smoking big cigars.

They told how they'd contrived to shirk
   Their wives with cunning wiles,
By saying how they had to work——
   Then—coming several miles
To lounge at a luxurious feast,
Without compunction—not the least—
   These bibulous old files!

The elder laughed, "It is my plan
   To scout wives' 'won'ts' and 'shan'ts.'"
The younger shouts, "When I say can,
   I heed no 'cant,' nor 'can'ts.'"
They chuckled o'er their ginger-beer,
O, it was terrible to hear
   These Uncles talk of Aunts!

The pie was pie'd, the pop was popped,
   Naught more could they devour,

With heavy heads asleep they dropped—
Such was the liquor's power!
To view the somnolescent pair
Strange things came up from everywhere,
And glared from every flow'r.

Now from the dinner-table mound
The Ants in millions swarmed,
Their serried masses hid the ground

In martial order formed;
And when their leaders showed the way,
Charging the Uncles as they lay,
  Their carcases they stormed.

The Northern army took the head
  And upmost part of each,
The Middle army—they were red—
  Seized all within their reach;
The Southern force invaded boots,
Advancing, then, by various routes,
  They mounted to the breach.

* * * * *

The man who dealt in pies and pops,
  At dawn found, strewn with plants,
Two corpses, lying near a copse,
  He knew them by their pants.
He wept! They'd ne'er return to pay!
Lifeless, but beautiful they lay,
  Two Uncles killed by Ants.

THE NEW HISTORY OF

CHAPTER XIII.

THE BLACKBERRY FEAST AT KIND MR. MERTON'S—TOMMY'S BIRTHDAY, AND WHAT HAPPENED. THIS CONTAINS ALSO STORY THE SEVENTH.

It happened about this time, that Mr. and Mrs. Merton requested the pleasure of Mr. Barlow's company to luncheon, and begged a holiday for his two pupils on occasion of the annual blackberry gathering, which they were holding in honour of Tommy's birthday, when a great number of his young friends would be present.

Mr. Barlow accepted the hospitable invitation, and never doubting but that several of the young gentlemen's parents would be also at Tiffin House, carefully filled his pockets with his scholastic cards, which informed the world how he was "*the* Tutor, par excellence, for unmanageable Boys, and how he could offer, to the most unruly, the advantage of a quiet home and perfect discipline. Taming for twenty pounds a Term. Terms vary." These cards were of a thin texture, and were covered with an adhesive substance at the back, so that he could readily and easily affix them to door-posts, to hats, to umbrellas, and indeed to any part of a person, or a place, which seemed to him to offer an effective spot for the display of this useful information.

Master Tommy appeared in a new suit of clothes,

consisting of blue jacket and brass buttons, white trowsers and vest, a little white hat, white silk gloves, shoes with buckles, and coloured socks, that made him the envy and admiration of all beholders.

Harry was more solidly but less gorgeously attired. He had on a plain brown jacket, yellow vest, and neat corduroy trowsers, kept tightly over his highlow boots with stout straps, whose force was resisted by a force applied above by a pair of equally strong braces. He wore a large white collar, and cotton gloves, carried an umbrella, and his head was adorned with a beaver hat, which with the greatest possible care he had brushed the wrong way. Just as they were about to enter the drawing-room, Harry asked Tommy if they had not better sit down and cool themselves after the walk, to which, Tommy, who was not a little particular about his appearance, readily assented, without observing that on the chair which Harry politely handed to him, there were laid, of course by the merest accident, a mulberry and a strawberry. Harry now occupied his friend's attention by busying himself about the set of his tie, the curl of his hair, and other matters of a like nature, for which Tommy expressed himself vastly grateful to his friend, who indeed observed, that it was a great gratification to him that his friend should bear a distinguished appearance, and be the cynosure of all eyes, while he himself would be content to hear his praises resound throughout the room.

They were now ushered into the drawing-room, where a large and gay company were assembled. On Tommy's walking down the room and making a superb bow, a general titter arose from those who were, for the moment, deprived of the inexpressible pleasure of seeing his face. To these however he turned himself, when a similar sound of suppressed laughter arose from those to whom so recently he had been making his courtesies. As for poor little Harry he was almost purple in the face, through his efforts to repress his feelings.

"Poor fellow," thought Tommy to himself, as he strutted about from one lady to another, and caught an occasional glimpse of his friend; "he little knows how they are all laughing at his awkward manner and vulgar appearance, and he himself seems, luckily for him, to be joining in the jest."

It was not until, at the request of his parents, Master Tommy had mounted on a table to declaim *My name is Norval*, (which he premised, "as you have not already heard it, I will now proceed to recite,") that the wrapt auditory burst out into an immoderate fit of laughter, and Mrs. Merton seizing her son round the waist, dashed with him from the room, followed closely by her agonised husband and the country practitioner, who began pulling from his pocket his case of surgical instruments as he rushed out at the drawing-room door.

During their absence the suspense was almost intolerable, and Harry, who could not behold the moist eyes of the ladies without being deeply affected, retired behind the laurel bushes, and roared with laughter.

When he returned to the saloon, Tommy was

back again among them, alive and well, and attired in a bran new pair of trowsers of a rich Jamaica pattern, woven out of the finest silk, and was offering his arm, with all the grace and politeness of a Louis Quinze, to his partner, whom he was to escort into the luncheon-room.

During this meal, Mr. Barlow, who was the life and soul of the merry party, found several convenient opportunities of distributing his cards among the visitors. He stuck them on the rims of the plates, on ladies' fans, on the bald pate of an elderly gentleman, "who," he said, "would find his (Mr. Barlow's) educational system, good for his *heir*." And as he had, with sundry significant glances, intimated that he was reserving his choicest anecdote until after the withdrawal of the ladies, upon the fair portion of the company quitting the apartment, Mr. Barlow complied with the general request of the gentlemen, and said " the present circumstances remind me of the story of *The Hermit and the Shrimp*,"—here the bald-headed gentleman applied his ear-trumpet and leant forward—" which as you have none of you heard it, I will now proceed to narrate."

Story the Seventh.

The Hermit and the Shrimp.

HE Hermit Koprokopos once met a young man working in the desert. Inducing him to pause in the midst of his toil, he thus addressed him: "My friend," said the venerable man, "why dost thou dig here?"

The young man answered that it was because he liked it.

"For what," asked the Hermit, "dost thou dig?"

"Pleasure," answered the young man, betaking himself once more to his work.

"And at what depth dost thou think to find pleasure?" inquired the Hermit.

"Down among the shrimps," answered the youth, who was already nearly up to his neck in sand.

"True," replied the Hermit benignly, "that is where thou wilt indeed find Pleasure. Dig on, and do not let *me* disturb thee."

Then he went his way, wondering no more that a young man should dig for shrimps in the desert, "for," said the venerable Hermit, "Pleasure is in this world as the Shrimp in the Desert."

"Which saying," added Mr. Barlow, "passed into a proverb amongst the tribes of the Go-to-Bedouin Arabs, only that they have never yet understood the meaning of the word Shrimp."

"The proverb travelled subsequently to other lands, where, strangely enough, the Shrimp was lost sight of, and the Crab substituted in its place. In more modern times the proverb, transmitted from the East, has been entirely lost in the West, nothing remaining of the original, from which the Shrimp has been entirely obliterated, except the confused jumble expressed in the name of the Hermit Crab.

"This evidently is a reminiscence of the old proverb, because, *firstly*, there never was a Hermit of the name of Crab; *secondly*, Crabs walk sideways and Hermits don't; *thirdly*, there never was a Hermit who was a Crab; *fourthly*, there was only one crabbed Hermit, and he lived on crab apples, wrote a book on Cidereal Observations of the sign Cancer, and never made a proverb, or a charade, in his life, and so it couldn't be he."

All Mr. Merton's guests were so highly pleased with this story, that, on Mr. Barlow's offering to give them two or three more of the same sort, they would not on any account hear of his again troubling himself so soon after his recent effort, which, they were good enough to say, they were certain he might possibly equal, but could never surpass. The old gentleman with the ear trumpet, who had been in convulsions of laughter during the narration, and invariably in the wrong places, now vowed he had never heard anything so good since he'd been stone deaf, a calamity, he informed them, of which he had never felt the affliction less than now. Mr. Barlow diffidently remarked that the last observation reminded him of the story of —— But at this juncture Mrs. Merton sent in to inquire if the gentlemen were not coming to join them at croquet, whereupon their host gallantly led the way to the lawn, whither all his guests followed with the utmost alacrity, leaving only Mr. Barlow, whom the deaf gentleman insisted upon detaining for at least another half hour, as he particularly wanted to try if he could catch any of the points of Mr. Barlow's story which he would be good enough to repeat to him. Mr. Barlow now commenced re-telling the story of the Hermit in the deaf-and-dumb alphabet on his fingers, which, as he had forgotten some of the most useful letters, occupied the greater part of the afternoon.

CHAPTER XIV.

THE SPANISH BULL-FIGHT, AS ARRANGED BY HARRY SANDFORD FOR THE AMUSEMENT OF TOMMY AND HIS YOUTHFUL COMPANIONS.

DURING the afternoon, Harry, who had received, as he informed them, some private information, proposed to the party of young gentlemen that they should come and see a Spanish Bull-fight, which, however, "they must keep," he said, "a profound secret from the elder guests." He then collected a shilling apiece from the little party, and led the way, through the meadows, to a field, not very far distant from Farmer Sandford's house.

Here they encountered a poor minstrel, whose face was perfectly black, and who was dressed in so quaint a garb as to excite the merriment of the youthful party. He informed them that his name was Johnson, and that, with his banjo, he was on his way to some races, which were to take place in the neighbourhood. He entertained them with several songs in his own peculiar dialect, and was proceeding to go round among them in order to receive such contributions as their charity might place in his hat, when Master Harry, who had been waving his red pocket-handkerchief for some time, suddenly cried out that the Spanish bull-fight was now about to commence, and having opened the gate of an adjoining paddock, he nimbly retired behind it, as a fine bull rushed from the inclosure, and, finding himself unrestrained, made at once for the place where Master Merton and his young associates were conversing with the intelligent negro. It is impossible to conceive the terror and dismay which instantly seized the crowd, who were now scattered over the plain, as they fled from the fury of the animal. The intelligent negro, who had just commenced to ask a conundrum, " Why is a———," was unable to finish the question, but mingling his shrieks with the outcries and lamentations that arose on all sides, seemed rooted to the spot by sudden terror.

His black face was in this instance his protection, and that colour which had subjected him to the scorn and derision of the crafty white men, now offered him as secure a concealment as if he had been possessed of the talisman used by the Invisible Prince in the fairy tale.

Not so fortunate was Master Merton; he happened to be full in the way which the bull had taken, and, while Harry was screaming with uncontrollable mirth at his friend's mishap, Master Tommy's foot slipped, and down he tumbled in the very path of the enraged pursuing animal. All who saw him imagined his fate inevitable, and Harry, with tears in his eyes and his hands to his sides, was still shrieking with laughter, when the bull, actuated by one of those strange freaks of madness, which will sometimes seize even the noblest animals, suddenly stopped short, and wheeling round in the direction whence the sounds of merriment proceeded, made with redoubled rage at this new object of his vengeance; and it is probable that, notwithstanding the agility with which he leaped over a five-barred gate, a feat in which he was the next minute successfully imitated by the bull, Master Harry would have paid the penalty of his extreme sense of the ludicrous, had not the poor black rushed like lightning to assist him, and, catching the bull's horns in his banjo, compelled him to turn his wrath in a fresh direction. In vain did the furious animal writhe and bellow; his redoubtable adversary soon swung himself on to his back, and using the banjo as a halter, defied all the creature's efforts to shake him off.

At this juncture, Farmer Jenkins, to whom the field belonged, came upon the spot, with a party of able-bodied labourers, who, throwing a well-twisted rope round the nigger's body, soon dragged him from his seat.

Farmer Jenkins now upbraided the negro with being the cause of the present disaster, and commanded his men to bring him up at once before the magistrate, who, without listening to his defence, which he had arranged in a series of songs and conundrums, fined him forty shillings or two months' imprisonment for trespassing, besides adjudging him to repay the honest farmer for damage done to both the field and the bull.

Being unable to defray so much expense, the unhappy Johnson was taken to the County Gaol, and Master Tommy subsequently wrote to the Governor of that establishment intimating his intention of prosecuting the negro on behalf of *The Society for the Prevention of Cruelty to Animals*, should he, upon his release from durance, ever again dare to venture into that neighbourhood.

To return, however, to the point where we left Tommy Merton on the ground. Harry, after clearing the gate, ran as fast as his legs could carry him, until happening to turn his head to see if the bull were still at his heels, he saw Mrs. Merton and Mr. Barlow coming towards him, accompanied by numerous servants and Master Tommy, who now seemed to be none the worse for his misadventure.

"That there Sandford, mum," exclaimed the ladies' maid, pointing at Harry, "he did it."

Mrs. Merton, who could scarcely have restrained herself from fainting every five minutes on Mr. Barlow's shoulder, had he not assisted her with a smelling-bottle of the strongest salts, without which he seldom travelled, now exclaimed with all the vehemence of which her excitable nature was capable,—

"Where is that abominable wretch as dared to take my own darling boy, out to a norrid bullfight?"

For though Mr. and Mrs. Merton were excessively wealthy people, yet long residence in the Island of Jamaica had done much for their letter "H," which, as it were, grew wild and luxuriantly among the flowers of speech which both Mr. and Mrs. Merton were in the habit of cultivating. Being, as Mr. Merton was proud of acknowledging, "self-made," they had little or no regard for their *h*antecedents, nor did they care for the position of their relatives; "but," as Mr. Merton sublimely remarked, "if we 'ave not *h*aspirates, at least we 'ave *h*aspirations, which," he would go on to explain to Master Tommy, "is a *h*epigram."

Tommy, then, on this occasion was not startled at his mother's excessive choler, which, indeed, he had often before witnessed ; but carried away by the feeling which was now so strongly manifested, by all the company present, against Harry Sandford, he sprang at his companion, and fetched him so sharp a blow, with his clenched fist, as changed the eye, to which it was applied, into a dissolving view of deepening hues.

To the surprise of all, who, whatever they might have thought of young Sandford as a low-born lout, would never have considered him a coward, Harry turned away, and, hiding his face in his right hand, while he held his left aloft, deprecatingly, towards his assailant, he only murmured in a heart-broken voice,—

"O Tommy! Tommy! a blow! That it should come to this!" here he pressed the injured part, as he continued; "O Tommy, Tommy, what would," here he raised his voice, " our beloved and revered tutor say ; what would your kind and truly noble father say had he seen your conduct this minute! Thank Heaven he has been spared——"

"No, he bean't," exclaimed a rough voice, which every one recognised as that of honest Farmer Sandford, for whom, as he carried a stout ash-stick and was followed by his famous bull-dog "Grumpy," everybody respectfully made way.

"No, he bean't; Mr. Merton coom'd oop t' field zame time as me an' the bull-poop did, an' I bain't goin to zee a zon o' mine put upon an' spurned by any zon o' the loikes o' you, zo I tellee. Dang my old zhirt buttons if I doan't thrash the lot o' you. Bite 'em, Grumpy!"

Mr. Sandford now made as though he would punch Mr. Merton's head, when Mrs. Merton, clasping Tommy in her arms, placed herself in front of her husband; and Mr. Barlow, advancing towards the justly incensed farmer, intimated that all could be rectified by a calm and dignified explanation.

Mr. Merton, on seeing that Grumpy had been silenced by a kick from his master's heavy boot, now came forth from his temporary concealment, and, interrupting his wife, as she was about, with the utmost endearments, to clasp her son to her bosom, said,—

"Hit his not now a time, mum, to give way to fondness for a child has 'as, I fear, hacted the basest and most wilest part what can never disgrace a 'uman bein'; and has can be honly a dishonour to 'is kind and doatin' parients. What," he continued, "was this what I 'eard when I come hup? What was this has I sor with my hown heyes? O Tommy, Tommy, 'ow hawful to think has you could be so beasly hungrateful has to go to strike the best and noblest of your frens!! Hand while he stood firm as a Christian Martha, see 'ow your unworthy conduck as plunged a ole famerly hinto grief and dismay!"

At this, Tommy could no longer contain himself, but burst into such a violent transport of crying, that Mrs. Merton, who protested against her "'usban's sewerity," caught her darlin' in 'er harms and carried 'im 'ome, accompanied by her friends and servants, who were glad to take the earliest opportunity afforded them of bidding farewell to Grumpy and Farmer Sandford, who was still twirling his thick stick, and eyeing Mr. Merton in a menacing fashion.

Mr. Merton, being occupied by such uneasy feelings, as we can imagine would disturb his ordinary equanimity on an occasion like the present, was agreeably surprised by the sudden interposition of Mr. Barlow, who once more undertook to settle the affair to their mutual satisfaction. Damage had been done to the field (for Farmer Jenkins was honest Mr. Sandford's tenant), and to the bull; the gate had been broken; the hedge injured; and, finally, the sad plight of Harry, who now complained of fearful pains in the head, and shootings in his jaws, and achings in his nasal bone, and for whom medical aid was evidently an absolute necessity. Mr. Merton at once gave Mr. Sandford a cheque for fifty pounds, and, on returning to his own house, insisted upon presenting Mr. Barlow with a handsome piece of plate and a gold snuff-box, in memory of the service rendered to him that day, and, moreover, would take no refusal of his invitation to dinner at Tiffin House.

CHAPTER XV.

DINNER OF A CONFIDENTIAL CHARACTER AT MR. MERTON'S. HARRY SANDFORD TELLS THE EIGHTH STORY.

AT dinner Mr. Merton made the severest reflections upon Tommy's "hinsolence hand hingratitude," and quoting from

Shakspeare, of whose works he was very fond, said,—

"' 'Ow 'arder than a serpent's tooth it is to 'ave a stingless child."

With numerous other pungent " 'ome-thrusts," to which poor Tommy could scarcely listen without fresh floods of tears.

"What partickly 'urts me," said Mr. Merton, "is to see him proceed to such repre'ensible hextremities without hany hadekit temptation; hextremities has, I fear, himplies a defect of goodness and generosity, wirtues has I'd ha' halways thought he'd ha' possessed in a 'igh degree."

"Neither," answered Mr. Barlow, on the appearance of the second bottle of old Madeira, "Neither am I at all convinced that your son is defishing—I should say, deficient in either. This wine is perfect. We broach the interior cask, as the poet has it."

"Poets don't 'ave nothin' like this 'ere, Mr. B.,"

said Mr. Merton with simple pride; "and it taint a hinferior cask at all, but bottled an' fust rate."

"Not 'inferior,' sir, but 'interior,' the quotation was Horatian. Which is a rhyme. Thank you, yes, I don't mind if I *do* take another glass."

"Now this 'ere Tommy! what's to be done with 'im? his he veak, hor vicked, hor both?"

"My dear sir," answered Mr. Barlow, "he is really of a noble disposition, and though——"

"'Is ungovernable hanger!" interrupted Mr. Merton, "'is wiolence and himpetuosity——"

"Are," said Mr. Barlow, taking him up at this point, "indeed fordimabble, I mean formidable. I don't think we can really manage—manage a fourth bol—"

"You mean bottle," said Mr. Merton, kindly.

"When," returned Mr. Barlow, with dignity, "I don't know wha' mean, you're at lib'ty t' c'rreckmer. I have known sev'ral inst'ces of young boys com' to me—unmange'ble—boys, who 've become phos'phorus, I sh'd say, ph'los'-phers, models of virtuesh and temp'ransh, orn'-mentsh for fire-stove and soshi'ty, only by tending one single—mor'l—lecture."

"Wash thash?" inquired Mr. Merton, lifting his head up from the table.

"It'sh," said Mr. Barlow, who was beginning to nod, and whose eyes were closing for more than a minute at a time, a habit which, with him, be-tokened deep thought; "it'sh a shtos'—sshtory—which ashyou've not heard it, I will p'ceed t' re'rate. You must know then—"

The heat of the room now proved too much for the two gentlemen after the excitement of recent events, and they succumbed to a drowsy feeling, which overpowered them so effectually, that Mr. Barlow could not reach his house that night, but was obliged to set off with Tommy, as early as circumstances would allow, the following morning. On their road they met Harry Sandford (whose eye appeared to be quite well), who "as neither of them heard it," or indeed at that moment, evinced any desire of becoming better acquainted with it, proceeded to narrate to them a story, which he said, seemed applicable to the present occasion. "I call it," he said, "*The Hermit and the Dessert.*"

Story the Eighth.

The Hermit and the Dessert.

A HERMIT who had lived for forty years on crusts of bread and eggshells, once came across a young man carrying fruits.

"For what purpose are these, my son?" inquired the holy man.

"For the desserts of several people in the town, my father," answered the youth.

"We seldom get our deserts," said the Hermit, gravely; "and, therefore, it will be no loss to these good folks if I consume the contents of the basket."

Whereupon he sat down and commenced eating

all the plums, gooseberries, currants, and raspberries.

The boy ran quickly to his employer, and told him what had befallen him.

His employer set out for the spot. Being arrived there, they found nothing but the empty pannier before the door of the Hermitage, which was now hermetically sealed.

The employer never recovered his fruits; neither did the Hermit.

On uncorking the Hermitage, some years afterwards, they found a little crust, and an agreeable perfume. Nothing more.

    *   *   *   *   *

They had now arrived at Mr. Barlow's, where they were to recommence those studies which the events of the last two days had interrupted.

CHAPTER XVI.

OF THE SAD ILLNESS OF MR. BARLOW, AND THE KINDNESS OF HIS PUPILS. HIS GRATITUDE. THE NINTH STORY.

FOR three days after the dinner at Mr. Merton's, Mr. Barlow was very unwell, and, indeed, by the order of Doctor Healwell, the physician, he was compelled to remain in bed, with the window blinds down. During this time the conduct of both Harry and Tommy was remarkable for its humanity, forbearance, and extreme politeness. They never banged a door loudly; never beat drums nor blew trumpets; never sat upon the keyboard of the grand piano, nor rang the bells, nor shouted up and down the stairs; they never screamed nor whistled; never kicked the pans and crockery about in the kitchen, which was directly under the sick-room where Mr. Barlow lay; they never once, in short, made any sort of noise, without immediately running up-stairs, and knocking at their beloved tutor's door, to express their compunction at having disturbed him, and to implore his forgiveness.

Mr. Barlow, being no less inclined towards justice than he was towards mercy, and whose patience during his illness was most exemplary, replied, feebly, that he forgave them most heartily for their acts, whether premeditated, or unintentional, at the same time remarking, in an undertone, to himself, as he again turned his throbbing head towards the wall, " I protest that I pardon their guilt, and I would that it were possible to remit, in full, such consequences as must ensue when I am once more well and strong."

Tommy and Harry now applied themselves assiduously to the study and practice of medicine; "for," observed Harry, thoughtfully, "it may so chance that either you or I, Master Tommy, might be prostrated by such an illness as has attacked our dear tutor ; and if we were obliged, for want of other assistance, to nurse one another, would it not be highly advantageous for each one to know, precisely, what the other was giving him as medicine, and whether the treatment was judicious or the contrary ?"

Tommy admitted that the acquisition of such a science was indeed most useful, and, whenever they were entrusted by the physician with his prescriptions, they were able to seize the opportunity of adding practical results to their experience.

They rubbed in the draughts which Mr. Barlow had to take every three hours, and gave him his lotion to drink, which they, having ascertained the medicinal property of certain vegetables, thoughtfully rendered more palatable by the infusion of one teaspoonful of decoction of cabbage-water, which Harry had obtained from the kitchen, during the momentary absence of the cook.

"We must not," said Tommy, with tears in his eyes, "leave any remedy untried in order that our beloved tutor may speedily be restored to health, which, he has often told us, is the greatest blessing that Providence can bestow."

After a grave consultation, Harry and Tommy now determined to try the effect of the cold water cure on Mr. Barlow. Taking advantage of his sleep, which they had humanely rendered more sound by the administration of a few grains of a powerful opiate, they carefully bandaged him up in a couple of sheets, which they then proceeded to saturate, with the contents of a watering-pot, so carefully applied, that not a single spot remained dry.

At the end of a couple of hours, and just before the good physician's visit, they removed the compresses and rubbed their tutor's still insensible form with coarse towels and flesh brushes, hold-

ing him up by the heels, pummelling his chest, and omitting none of those means by which drowning men are usually restored to consciousness.

As they were pouring brandy down his throat Mr. Barlow gradually revived. The doctor now arrived, and pronounced a crisis to be at hand; indeed the eminent physician appeared not a little astonished at the state in which he had found his patient, and which, he owned, had entirely baffled even his skill, and was totally at variance with all the precedents with which his experience of similar maladies had hitherto furnished him.

Tommy and Harry now determined to do their best to merit the doctor's approbation, and ascertaining that vital warmth was absolutely indispensable in order to ensure the invalid's recovery, they contrived to fill the warming-pan with blazing live coals, and this instrument they introduced with such effect, into Mr. Barlow's bed, that he leapt out of it with so much energy and agility, as to cause the utmost consternation in the minds of his young benefactors, who, running pell-mell out of the room, and down the staircase, announced to the terrified domestics, that their revered tutor had gone suddenly mad, and was pursuing them with the warming-pan, with which he had threatened to take their lives.

The butler, who was a man of intrepid courage, immediately ran out of the house, and, having summoned some farm labourers armed with pitchforks, the parish clerk, and one of the rural police force, made his way to Mr. Barlow's chamber, where the constable, who was allowed by the butler to precede the party in his official capacity, cautiously opened the door, and called upon Mr. Barlow in the Queen's name to surrender, "or," added the parish clerk, who was close behind him, "for ever after hold your tongue." Receiving no answer they burst into the room, and throwing themselves, all at once, upon the unfortunate gentleman, bound him securely, and laid him on his bed, into which, indeed, he had been on the point of stepping, when thus rudely disturbed.

Harry could not see his tutor thus used without exhibiting the liveliest concern. He suffered agonies of laughter, and rolled on the floor of the passage in such convulsions as caused Tommy considerable alarm for his friend's safety.

In the meantime, the butler had gone to the house of the nearest Justice of the Peace, who, on repairing to the scene of the recent excitement, warmly approved the conduct of the police officer, whom he forthwith dismissed from the force.

Tommy and Harry were now no longer permitted to visit their tutor, for whom a regular attendant was provided by the doctor, who indeed could scarcely restrain his gratitude to the two boys for all they had done to assist him in his arduous duties. "You will," observed the kindly doctor to them, "no doubt, meet with the reward which is justly due to your merits, and concerning which Mr. Barlow and myself have already agreed. You will be rejoiced to hear that he is gradually returning to health."

Harry and Tommy managed, by a powerful effort, to control their very natural feelings on receiving this intelligence, and spent the remainder of the day in splitting up the choice collection of canes which they had found in Mr. Barlow's study, and in digging certain deep holes in the garden, where, with many expressions of esteem and respect, they buried the three apple-twig, and birch rods, which their careful tutor had provided for the winter season.

On the tenth night of his convalescence, the two boys were aroused, from their sleep, by the butler, and summoned to the bedside of their beloved tutor, who, propped up by pillows, addressed them with the following solemn exhortation :—

" A boy," said he, while the butler stood by, attempting to stifle the emotion which found vent in choking sobs, " A boy, who has once learned to feel the certainty of the laws of molecular action, so long as he retains his mental soundness, cannot relapse into that state of vague indifference about facts which characterises many uneducated persons, nor can he lose the habit of exactitude of conception and statement, to which he is compelled by practice in chemical reasoning, It is undoubtedly well that everyone should know something of the structure and functions of his own body——"

Here Tommy, apologising for the interruption, begged to be allowed to return to his room, where he would assume, he said, such articles of apparel as might enable him to listen to his tutor's discourse with less danger of catching cold than he was at present incurring. In this request Harry also joined, and they would have retired from the apartment, but that the butler was standing before the door, which, indeed, he had locked, apparently listening, in wrapt attention, to the words of his beloved employer.

"As for what you allege," returned Mr. Barlow, "I will presently see that you suffer in no respect from lack of such warmth as it is in my power to apply to your corporeal frames."

At the mention of "frames," Harry glanced at his young friend, who hung his head, somewhat abashed, while Mr. Barlow resumed.

"I was saying that everyone should be acquainted with the structure and functions of his own body; because he is thereby better able to take care of himself, and to understand how to preserve himself by reasonable precautions against some of the recognised causes of pain and suffering."

So saying Mr. Barlow produced, from under the bed clothes, an entirely new birch rod of remarkable size and prodigious strength, while, at the same instant, the butler drew from out of his coat sleeve a supple cane of some thickness, the like of which neither Master Tommy, nor Harry, had ever met with before.

"I observe," continued Mr. Barlow, "that you are both slightly shivering, and as I would never lose an opportunity of combining instruction with amusement, I would have you to notice the chemical change which is the essence of vital phenomena; and I trust that concerning the relation between the production of animal heat and of external motion, you will this night receive such indelible impressions as no lapse of time will be able to entirely efface."

Mr. Barlow now bade his pupils remain quiet, and instantly jumping from the bed (when for the first time they perceived that he was clothed in his day dress), with an alacrity and vigour

which perfectly amazed them, took Tommy by the nape of his neck, and informing him that he considered the birch most suitable for him, while the bamboo would be fitter for Harry, was proceeding, according to his favourite system, to practically exemplify his recent lecture on animal heat and its sources, when Harry exclaimed,—

"Stop, sir, I entreat. You have mentioned the bamboo. Pray, sir, what is a bamboo?"

Mr. Barlow could not refuse compliance with this request, and, exchanging his birch for the cane, while he committed Tommy to the butler, he himself undertaking the instruction of Master Harry, thus replied,—

"The bamboo, my dear Harry, is an Indian reed, full of dark spots, which look like joints. The bamboo sometimes grows to the height of a hundred feet."

"And what, sir," asked Harry, shrinking away into a corner, and putting up his elbow in order to lighten as far as possible the shock of the first stroke; "and what, sir, is their principal use?"

"The ancients," answered Mr. Barlow, leisurely poising the cane, and eyeing Master Harry all over, on the principle of natural selection, "the ancients valued them for their sweet juice * * *"

"Oh! sir—please——"

"Which," continued Mr. Barlow, firmly, "served (*whack*) them (*whack*) for (*whack*) sugar (*swish—whack*)."

"O!—if you—please—O, *sir!*"

"And," said Mr. Barlow, with marked emphasis, and, as it were, underlining each word with a stroke, "*the* (*shwack*) *young* (*shwack*) *shoots* (*shwack*) *they* (*shwack*) *pickled!* (*shwack—shwack, boo hoo hoo!!*)"

The butler in the meantime had not allowed himself to be an inactive spectator of the scene, though, as Master Tommy had managed to whisper in his ear, that he would give him a sovereign before he went to bed that night, if he would not flog him, he so performed his part, as also, indeed, did Master Tommy, who cried and howled more vociferously than did even Master Harry, that Mr. Barlow thought it more prudent to stop, than to allow the continuance of an uproar which would, in all probability, deprive his neighbours of that well-earned repose to which the labours of the day had entitled them.

Mr. Barlow now betook himself to the sofa, and having refreshed himself with a glass of sherry and a sandwich, asked them, whether, in their opinion, they had had enough.

"Indeed, sir," said Harry, "I have. But I cannot undertake to answer for Tommy, who is, I fancy, of a less contented disposition than myself."

Tommy, however, protested that he could not on any account think of further trespassing upon either Mr. Barlow's, or the butler's kindness, both of whom he was sure must stand in need of rest.

Mr. Barlow thanked him for his consideration, and observed that his conduct reminded him of the story of *The Sage and the Onion*, which, said he, "as neither of you have heard it, I will proceed to narrate. There is, however, no necessity to detain Binney, who can go to bed."

The honest butler, to whom Mr. Barlow had thus given permission to retire, made a grateful reverence to his master, and after a vain effort to attract the attention of Master Tommy, withdrew.

THE NEW HISTORY OF

Mr. Barlow, having taken another glass of wine, now commenced

Story the Ninth.
The Sage and the Onion.

SAGE was once out walking, when he met an elderly man weeping bitterly for the death of his uncle, who had left him two hundred thousand pounds, of which he refused to bestow a moiety on the Sage.

"Tears are no proof of sorrow," quoth the Sage; and forthwith producing from his robe an onion, he handed it round to the bystanders, who, smelling, began also to weep bitterly.

After this they fell upon the man, and beat him soundly. The chief lawyers, too, declared his estate confiscate, on account of his hypocrisy, and made over a portion to the Sage, on whom also was bestowed the title of *The Worthy*. Subsequently, a coat-of-arms was granted to him, exhibiting one onion, rampant, on a field, proper, and, underneath, the motto

L'Onion fait la force.

"Now," said Mr. Barlow, "you may go to bed. And remember the treatment which you have received from a poor invalid, in return for all your kindness to him during his affliction. Good-night and bless you."

144   THE NEW HISTORY OF

CHAPTER XVII.

OF HARRY AND TOMMY'S GREAT GARDENING OPERATION.
MR. BARLOW TELLS THEM THE TENTH STORY.

OMMY was now making great progress in the use of the hoe, with which Mr. Barlow had entrusted him. He no longer hit Harry on the head with it, or chopped Mr. Barlow's shins when he happened to be standing near at hand.

Both boys became so thoroughly imbued with the true spirit of agricultural industry, that they had taken to pickaxes in their leisure moments, a recreation however, which Mr. Barlow, on due consideration, thought fit to restrain within certain limits. Now it so chanced that adjoining Mr. Barlow's ground was that of the indefatigable Mr. Texter, his neighbour, who had the good fortune to possess a sufficiently well-stocked garden, and an orchard filled with the finest fruit trees. He had also a beautiful pond, full of gold and silver fish, and very fine carp, which when Tommy and Harry looked over the hedge, they were able to see swimming about, and sometimes showing their noses above water, among the lilies, when, as quick as lightning, and with the true instinct of a genuine sportsman, Harry would take, with a simple stone, so good an aim, that the adventurous denizen of the water would be glad enough to withdraw to a shady spot, where he would be less likely to court observation. Tommy had often eaten of the fruit of the orchard, and had thought it delicious, though, with innate modesty, he had neither confided his opinion to

Harry, nor had he expressed it before Mr. Barlow. The contemplation of these apples, plums, and cherries, led him to think that it would be a great improvement to Mr. Barlow's garden, if he had a few of these trees, which Harry, to whom he proposed the idea, pointed out could be easily transplanted, without any sort of injury to the trees themselves.

Mr. Barlow on being finally consulted on the matter, told them that "doubtless a few apples, plums, and greengages would present a pretty effect on his ground, and would be of no slight service to the tart and jam department of his limited household; but," he added, "you must remember, my dear young friends, that as the trees are Mr. Texter's and not mine, I can neither give, nor withhold, directions for their removal." Transplanting, he went on to assure his attentive pupils, he considered a most useful and entertaining process, and he further admitted that he saw them, with pleasure, occupying themselves with pursuits at once so noble and so serviceable to mankind. For his part, it was a matter of regret to him, that his good neighbour, Mr. Texter, should unfortunately be absent at this time, so that he could not witness the labours of his young friends, which he would, Mr. Barlow felt certain, be the first to estimate at their true value.

Exhilarated by this praise, Tommy and Harry visited the orchard one lovely moonlight night, and without making any special appointment with Mr. Texter's gardener, whom, after a hard day's work and an evening at the tavern, it would have been cruel to have aroused from his well-earned repose, they at once selected six of the healthiest-looking trees they could find, which they now proceeded to transplant to Mr. Barlow's garden in the following manner :—

They both took their spades, and very carefully dug the trees up, without injuring the roots, then they dragged them along the ground, and by the aid of a ladder, and some stout ropes, they soon hoisted the trees over the low garden wall.

Then they dug large holes in the places where they chose the trees should stand, and very carefully broke the earth to pieces that it might lie light upon the roots. Then they planted the trees in their new positions, and christened them with these names, Harry, Tommy, Mr. Barlow, Texter, and Texter's Gardener. When this had been done to their entire satisfaction, they returned to Texter's garden in order to restore the ground to its former neatness, as they knew Mr. Texter to be a particularly orderly and tidy person. This they soon managed with the aid of a watering-pot, and lightly trampling on the earth which they had disturbed.

Mr. Barlow who, in his nightcap, had been a not unmoved spectator of this scene, from his bedroom window, could not restrain a feeling of gratitude on beholding the complete success of this his beloved pupils' first attempt at horticulture on anything like a grand scale.

Nor did they bound their attention here. Noticing on the following day that the ground, where the new trees were, was very dry and arid, they conceived the idea of irrigating Mr. Barlow's land with the water from Mr. Texter's pond. They now laboured hard for several days to form a new channel which should lead the water near the roots of the trees. This they contrived to do without any assistance from either Mr. Texter, who was away, as it was believed, in Germany, or from his gardener, who, during his master's absence was giving himself a holiday.

Mr. Barlow saw them employed in this manner with the greatest satisfaction. He encouraged them, while they worked, with stories of the most instructive character, and when, one afternoon, Tommy and Harry showed themselves somewhat overcome with their exertions, Mr. Barlow produced from his pocket some dry biscuits, with which he regaled his young friends, recommending them to moisten the repast, with some of the water, which had already commenced to dribble in from Mr. Texter's pond.

"This," said Mr. Barlow, when he had refreshed

himself with a luscious peach, a sponge cake, and some light beverage which he carried with him in a soda-water bottle, "reminds me of the story of *The Magistrate and the Elephant*, which as you have not yet heard it, I will at once proceed to narrate."

CHAPTER XVIII.

Story the Tenth.

The Magistrate and the Elephant;
or,
Duty and Pleasure.

A Moral Ballad.

A MELANCHOLY Magistrate
Once sat and scratched his sad pole;
He cried, "I've never learnt to skate,
I wish I was a tadpole.
Yet tadpoles do not skate, but they
To learn have the entire day."

An Elephant who chanced just then
To issue from a jungle,
Addressed him thus: "O best of men,
This here will be a bungle.

Why envy tadpoles, carp, or tench,
When you've a seat upon the bench?"

The Magistrate took off his wig,
　And sobbed, "I'm hurt to find
An animal like you so big,
　So dreadfully unkind.
Be gentle to my agëd pate,
You *can't* know *how* I want to skate."

The Elephant dropped from his eye
    A tear upon his trunk.
"Excuse me, reverend sir, if I
    Imagined you were drunk.
Then, prithee, tell me why you thus
About your skating make this fuss."

The Magistrate took out a book
    And said, "Just read this list,
It tells you all that I can do,
    From cricketing to whist.
At every sort of sport I'm great,
But yet, alas! I cannot skate.

If I could skate about a lake,
    Some prizes I might win."
"But ice," said Elephant, "may break,
    And then you'd tumble in;
When if you cannot swim, my friend,
Your skating and your life would end."

"That may be true or may be not,"
    The Magistrate replied;
"It quite depends, you see, on what
    May happen at the side.
For if they've buoys and lots of line,
Lives may be saved, and why not mine?

"I have with me of skates a pair,"
    The Elephant said. "Now

If you will hold on by a chair,
    To skate I'll show you how."
Here he began to imitate
The movement of the figure eight.

Then said the Magistrate, "I'll kneel
    And make a little hole;"
He took a gimlet, and the steel
    Enter'd his very sole.
"Now," quoth the Magistrate, "what next?"
The Elephant tho' looked perplexed.

Then thus the Elephant: "I'm pained
    To own"—he slightly coughed,
"That we can't skate, because it's rained,
    And now the water's soft.
But if you *will* take my advice,
You'll wait to skate until there's ice."

They waited all the summer through,
    Till February's end.

Then said the Magistrate, "Are you
   Aware, my worthy friend,
That if there doesn't come a frost,
I have my golden moments lost?"

The thoughtful Elephant replied,
   "You chose yourself to wait;
Why not contented be, and slide,
   I'm sure you'll never skate.
And sliding's really very nice,
But then again you *must* have ice."

"I will!" the Magistrate exclaimed.
   "You for your sense I thank,
Indeed, I feel I shall be blamed
   For staying on this bank,
When on my bench I should have been.
I must ask pardon of the Queen."

Then on his legs he tried to stand,
   The Elephant likewise,

He grasped his trunk with trembling hand,
  But neither could arise.
They'd grown so weak, that, down the bank
They rolled into the pond, and sank.

The waters closed above his head
  Ere he could touch the path—
*   *   *   *
Somehow he had got out of bed
  To skate upon his bath.

For magistrates are not exempt
From dreaming like as this one dreamt.

"The moral," said the Magistrate,
  "Is clear as legal French—
Pleasure is meant I see by Skate,
  And duty by the Bench ;
If for the former I neglect
The latter, what can I expect ?"

And so he worked and worked away,
  Much dreaded by his clerk,
And never took a holiday
  For any sort of lark,
He never from his bench would budge,
Until, at last, he was a Judge.

CHAPTER XIX.

SHOWING WHAT WAS THE RESULT OF MASTERS TOMMY
AND HARRY'S GREAT GARDENING OPERATION.

WHEN the Rev. Mr. Texter returned from his holiday, he was amazed at finding his pond almost drained, and the fish scarcely gaining a livelihood from the mud and weeds at the bottom.

As his gardener displayed signs of insobriety, and was totally unable either to explain the circumstance, or to account for his own conduct, except by pleading the really uncommon heat of the weather, Mr. Texter, who, though a man of great science and considerable research, having lately been reading a paper on *Temperature* to a Society of German Savans, could not do otherwise than discharge his servant, without paying him those wages, which his master asserted to have been forfeited by his intoxication, and for which, as this imputation was on the other hand, strenuously denied, the gardener brought an action, and won it, with heavy damages against his former employer for defamation of character. All this, the Reverend Mr. Texter, who was still deeply engaged on his work on *Temperature*, attributed, in a letter to the German Association, to the effect of the Heat of the moment. Nor did he omit, on this occasion, to corroborate one of his own pet theories of absorption, by recounting to this learned body, the extraordinary case of the sudden evaporation of all the water from a pond, which, a month ago, he had left full, to overflowing, in his own garden.

Mr. Barlow's orchard was by this time irrigated to such an extent, that, what had previously been soft and pleasant turf, was now little better than a swamp, from which there came forth, at night, so poisonous an exhalation, that the Inspector of Nuisances was ordered by the Government, to whom he had already reported the fact, to inquire into its cause. This led to the institution of a Commission, in which both Mr. Barlow and the Rev. Peter Texter were considerably interested.

The evidences of the boys' skill now soon became apparent, and Mr. Barlow's groom, who, having been obliged to suffer a reduction of wages since Masters Tommy and Harry had undertaken the garden, to tend which had been heretofore a portion of his duty, had undertaken odd jobs and piece work on Mr. Texter's domain, now positively swore to the presence of the six trees in Mr. Barlow's garden, which had, till lately, been in that of Mr. Texter, and further undertook to point out the reason for the miasma which had arisen from the marshy condition of his master's orchard.

Tommy and Harry now called on their tutor, and reminded him that he had witnessed their work from his bedroom window, and had contributed not a little, by his evident gratification, to the unlooked-for success of their undertaking.

Harry. Why, sir, the groom, had he possessed the tools, and the intelligence, might himself have performed this feat.

Tommy. I vow and protest that the Commissioners already are of opinion that it was *his* work, and not *ours*.

Mr. Barlow. Whether is it, then, more the part of true modesty to announce before all the world one's own share in a glorious enterprise, or to keep silence, while another receives the praise to which he is in no way entitled?

Tommy. I protest, sir, it seems nobler to let others discover for themselves the author of a great work, than that he should deprive himself of additional merit, by declaring his own excellence.

Harry. Besides, sir, as it was *we* who did it, under your superintendence, how impossible is it for anyone to absolutely prove that it is the deed of another person, who was never once on the spot.

This consultation decided them in preserving strict silence, and should they be obliged to speak at all on the subject, they settled rather to allow another to take all the honours, than to prefer their own just claims.

The Commissioners, after hearing the opinions of many eminent lawyers on the subject, concluded their labours at the end of a month, during which time the orchard had resumed its former condition, and the miasma had entirely disappeared.

CHAPTER XX.

WHAT HAPPENED TO MR. TEXTER. HARRY TELLS THE ELEVENTH STORY.

Mr. Texter now set on foot a subscription to defray the expenses of these proceedings, which had fallen mainly upon himself, and publicly announced in church that the offertory for the next half-year would be devoted to this purpose. Whereupon Mr. Barlow held a meeting of the vestrymen, and appealed to the Bishop of the diocese, who, in his next charge, highly reprobated the conduct of the indefatigable Mr. Texter, and on dining with him, during his visitation, severely reprimanded him, in private, for behaviour which could not but alienate from the Church such influential parishioners as Mr. Barlow, Mr. Merton, and Farmer Sandford; begging him, for the future, to confine his attention to scientific subjects, and the vices of the poor, for both of which he would find ample leisure.

Mr. Merton, in whose gift the living was, now requested the removal of Mr. Texter, who was soon after presented with a foreign curacy at a favourite German watering-place, which he not unwillingly accepted. On the last Sunday of his ministration in his English parish, he read the Commination service with so much unction, that the congregation surrounded the vestry after church, and would have subjected their revered pastor to considerable violence, but for the timely interposition of Mr. Barlow, to whose nephew Mr. Merton had now intrusted the living.

Tranquillity being once more restored, Mr. Barlow summoned his beloved pupils to his study and thus addressed them :—

"I cannot conceal from you, my little friends, that you have acted very ill in this affair. However, if you are really ashamed of your past conduct, I shall have the greatest pleasure in punishing you only with such severity as justice, tempered by mercy, absolutely demands at my hands."

Harry. Oh, sir, I should be the happiest creature in the world, if you would only flog Master Tommy instead of me. Will you be so kind as to do this, and you shall see how I will behave.

Mr. Barlow. Softly, Harry, softly. I will so far comply with your request, as to take his case first, and in order to prevent any unseemly struggles, you, who are stronger than he is, can hold him firmly down in the arm-chair.

Here Tommy burst into tears, and begged his friend, who could scarcely restrain his delight, to let him go. This, as Harry could not consent to do of his own accord, being, as he said, bound in honour to their tutor, Master Tommy now attempted to effect for himself; and in a few seconds Mr. Barlow, on returning from the cupboard where the apple-twig rod was usually kept, had the pleasure of seeing his little pupils mutually giving, and receiving, every unaffected mark of the warmest affection, until an accidental blow, delivered with more than ordinary accuracy, levelled Harry with the carpet. Tommy was now about to seize his companion's head with all the impetuosity of which he was capable, when Mr. Barlow intimated to him, in a striking and forcible manner, that a fallen adversary should rather inspire sentiments of pity, than of revenge.

After the application of vinegar and brown paper, Mr. Barlow, taking each by the hand, led them into the dining-room, where, while their beloved tutor partook of his frugal supper, Harry had the pleasure, at Tommy's request, of narrating to them a story, which up to that time neither he nor Mr. Barlow had heard.

"You must know, then," said Harry, "that the story which I shall now narrate——"

"In verse," said Mr. Barlow, taking a pickled walnut.

"In verse," assented Harry, giving Tommy a kick underneath the table.

"I vow and protest——" Tommy began, when Mr. Barlow begged that there might be no interruption to the harmony of the evening, and immediately called upon Harry to recite his ballad of *Don Ditto and the Dutchmen*.

CHAPTER XXI.

Story the Eleventh.

LEGEND OF

Don Ditto and the Dutchmen;
or,
The Dey and the Knight.

Don Ditto was as brave a knight
  As any knight in Spain,
He loved with Moors and Turks to fight,
  To cut and come again.

He hated much the Double Dutch,
  Because they were such boors,

And always thought the greatest sport,
A day among the Moors.

The Double Dutch too hated him,
Because he spoiled their trade,

And once when he'd gone out to swim
("Twas in the summer twilight dim)
Him prisoner they made.

Unto Algiers, with shouts and cheers,
    They brought him all the way,
And there the Christians saw, with tears,
    The Knight before the Dey.

But by the Dey there stood a girl,
    Who caught Don Ditto's eye,
And his caught hers, and in a whirl
    Their heads went rapidly.

She was the daughter of the Dey,
    (Katinka was her name),
With him she always had her way,
    For which he was to blame.

"And now," she cried, "O dearest pa,
    I prithee spare this youth."
The Dey replied, "I think you are
    In love." She said, "That's truth."

"I'll be a Christian," quoth the Dey,
"And you shall wed this maid,
If all my debts the Don will pay."
"I'm there," Don Ditto said.

The Dutchmen swore, that never more
They'd lend the Dey a rap.
They saw Don Ditto quit the shore,
Waving his feathered cap.

Part II.

DON DITTO went to Palestine, (Described in works of Kitto's,) And there his chain-mail-armour fine Was called a suit of Ditto's.

He rode about the desert red
    Until he met a Paynim,
He gave him one upon his head,
    And cried, " I think I've slain him."

Don Ditto rode from six to ten,
  All ready for a tussle ;
He met a lot of Mussulmen,
  But none were men of muscle.

He used to hide behind the rocks
  Until they got quite near him,
And then he would take off his socks
  That so they shouldn't hear him.

Upon the Paynim dog he'd fly,
  Or slily with a knife come,
Then raise the Christian battle-cry,
  " Your money or your life ! Come ! "

And thus he made of coin a heap,
  And in his bags he stored it,
He bought a lot of armour, cheap,
  Because he could afford it.

But Abou Al Effendi Sam,
    Swore by the holy Prophet,
He'd make Don Ditto into jam,
    And send him down to Tophet.

Effendi Sam at night stole out,
    While Ditto lay a-sleeping,
When there was nobody about,
    Save one, who watch was keeping.

Effendi to the teeth came armed,
    And creeping like an adder.
The secret watcher was alarmed
    To see this horrid shadder.

This secret watcher was a page
    Who'd joined Don Ditto lately—
His means allowed him to engage
    A boy, it looked so stately.

Effendi crazed, with arm upraised,
Was bent on doing murther,
When—ah!—he felt a sudden smart,
Something went through him like a dart,
And he did nothing further.

The boy to Ditto's thanks replied
  No word; he blushed far pinker
Than maidens do. "For you," he cried,
"I'd risk my life . . . I am your bride."
  She swooned. It was Katinka!

Don Ditto now recalled his vow,
And grateful knelt to thank her.
And so before the hour of noon,
They married, and their honeymoon
They spent at Salamanca.

CHAPTER XXII.

A SCHOOL-DAY OF STUDIES WITH MR. BARLOW.

PUNCTUALLY at nine o'clock, Mr. Barlow took his seat at a high desk which he had had specially made for educational purposes. It was fitted with a book-rest, an inkstand, a place for pens, and a small shelf for a couple of canes. A gong hung from a hook by the side, and this Mr. Barlow sounded, with so much vigour, that the neighbours at first used to shut their windows and hide the table-knives, under the impression that a fearful storm was imminent. Such too was the notion which its sound conveyed to Master Tommy and Harry, who ran away as fast as their little legs could carry them in order to seek shelter beneath the hospitable roof of Mrs. Brown, who had for years provided sweetstuff to the village children at remarkably low prices.

Becoming accustomed to the summons, they now took a delight in being so early in the study as to be able to sound the gong for themselves, or to assist their beloved tutor to discover the spot where the stick had been, by some chance, mislaid.

"We will now," said Mr. Barlow, "commence with English Grammar, and we will consider this morning the formation of the perfect, or past tense. What, my dear Harry, is the perfect of 'I weave?'"

Harry. " I wove."

Mr. Barlow. You are indeed right; and now, my dear Tommy, what is the perfect of "I leave ?"

Tommy. " I love."

Mr. Barlow. True. For I would not have you adopt the modern fashion which has made our language so difficult for civilised nations to learn. "Left" is the contrary of "right," and cannot be the past participle of "to leave;" nor can "I left" be the first person singular perfect tense of the same verb. If "I weave" makes "I wove," it is clear that "I leave" makes "I love," only let us write two little dots over it, to signify that the *o* is to be pronounced long.

Here Mr. Barlow drew the word Love on his black board with a piece of chalk, carefully placing two dots over the vowel, thus : " I leave, I löve." "We will now continue. Conjugate 'to give' on my plan."

Harry. "I give, Thou give, He give. *Perfect,* I gave."

Mr. Barlow. Very correct, indeed. Let me hear, Tommy, what you make of the verb " to live " ?

Tommy. " I live, Thou live, He live. *Perfect,* I lave."

Mr. Barlow. I am glad to find that you have so thoroughly mastered my instructions. You will go up two places in your own class, and Harry will take three in his. I shall have great pleasure in informing your parents, that you are, each, respectively at the head of his class. Take care, however, lest you be deposed, and so lose the eminence you have attained. Give me now (*to Harry*) Master Sixth Form, Upper School, the perfect of the verb " I advise."

Harry. " I advöse."

Mr Barlow (*to Tommy*). And now, Master Captain of the Fourth Form, Upper Division. give me the perfect of " I crow."

Tommy. " I crew."

Mr. Barlow. Of " I flow."

Tommy. " I flew."

Mr. Barlow. "I mow."

Tommy. "I mew."

Mr. Barlow. Very good. The plural of "Mouse."

Harry. "Mice."

Mr. Barlow. Of "House," "Grouse," and the past participle of "to chouse," and "to souse."

Harry. "*Singular,* house; *plural,* hice," and "grouse, grice; chouse, chice; souse, sice." Thus "soused pig," a very excellent dish, should be correctly "siced pig."

Mr. Barlow. What are proper names?

Tommy. Names such as Tommy, Harry, Barlow, and so forth.

Mr. Barlow. And improper names?

Harry. You fool, you donkey, you unmitigated blackguard, you——

Mr. Barlow (*removing his cane from the shelf*). That will, I think, be sufficient for the present, unless——

Harry. Nay, sir, I was but replying to your question.

Mr. Barlow. You will go down three places, and you are fined sixpence, which you will at once hand over to me, in order (*poising his cane*) to stay further proceedings.

The fine was immediately paid.

Mr. Barlow. Give me now, Master Tommy, an example of what you understand by a relative pronoun.

Tommy. My uncle.

Mr. Barlow. Right. Now oblige me with your view of possessive pronouns.

Tommy. " Mine, thine, hern, and hisn." *Example,* " What's mine ain't thine, and what's hern ain't hisn."

Mr. Barlow. Conjugate the verb " ain't."

Tommy. "I ain't, you ain't, he ain't," &c.; and *imperfect,* " I bain't." *Perfect,* " I warn't."

Mr. Barlow. Very good. You will this morning come out of the Upper Fourth Form, and be placed in the Second Division Lower Remove, of which I trust you will henceforth be a distinguished ornament. It is customary for a boy thus elevated to present the master with a fee of one shilling for raising him to that degree; unless, indeed (*taking up the cane again*), he should prefer——

Tommy, however, with many fervent protestations of gratitude, at once presented Mr. Barlow with the amount requested, who thereupon called up the History Class.

Mr. Barlow. Who was Ketchup?

Harry. A well-known Turk, who invented a sauce of that name, and was an intimate friend of the Egyptian Cheops.

Mr. Barlow. Where is Sassafras?

Tommy. An island in the Levant, celebrated for its pack-thread and dry walnuts.

Mr. Barlow. What do you know of Cadmus?

Harry. He was the originator of omnibuses, and stood on the step behind. Hence the derivation of cad. He also invented that useful article of furniture known as the bed-post.

Mr Barlow. What was the cause of the Second Mithridatic War?

Tommy. Plums.

Mr. Barlow. Who was William Rufus?

Harry. An eminent architect who built the New Forest.

Mr. Barlow. Mention all you know of the rise and fall of the Great Mogul.

Tommy. He was a thick white man, dressed in black sarsnet, with a resinous piece on the top of his head, which he regularly every morning washed over with a soft solution of benzoin. When he had tied up his bags, he proceeded to the town of Bantam, in Syria, where he showed his gums to the people. These they bought with avidity, and determined henceforth to stick to him. He taught them many arts with which they had been previously acquainted, such as the curing of diseases in fish, the use of the snuff-box, and the properties of the tea-urn. After this he made Borax his prime minister, and generalissimo of his forces, consisting chiefly of Dutch Cochineal, and a gentleman of a greenish colour, who carried an obelisk which had been hitherto much neglected. He lived to an old age, and was destroyed in the reign of James the First by a hackney coach which rolled over him, and he was buried at the expense of the inhabitants of Calcutta, in the North Caribbean Sea.

Mr. Barlow. Is this all you know about this remarkable man ?

Tommy. Not entirely; but should you wish for any further particulars, I shall be happy, for the consideration of a small sum, to impart additional information, which, otherwise, I should have been inclined to consider as strictly private and confidential.

Mr. Barlow. I will remind you of your promise presently; in the meantime, Harry, can you inform me what were the principal tortures used in the Middle Ages ?

Harry. Indeed, sir, I have long since made them my especial study. They were the Thumbscrew, the Maiden, the Rack, the Little Ease, the Painful Tooth Extractor, the Penetrating Spike, the Joke Incisor used in Scotland, the Nail Drawer, the Head Twister, the Toe Wrencher, the

Nose Lopper, the Slow Roaster, with many others, models of which I have not yet been able to make.

Mr. Barlow. Have you, with your most useful knowledge of carpentering, been able to construct anything like the rack, which I suggested you should make in this room?

Harry. Indeed, sir, I have; and I think you will find it most suitable for the purpose for which it was constructed.

Mr. Barlow now drew back a curtain which had formerly concealed his boot-rack, but which by removing the boots, had been ingeniously formed into a simple rack by Harry's contrivance.

Mr. Barlow (while Harry adjusted the ropes and turned the screws). Now, Master Tommy, I shall be able to ascertain, by the application of what was termed the Question, whether you have, or have not, anything further to relate concerning the private history of the Great Mogul.

Tommy now vowed and protested that he had told all he knew of the matter, and indeed offered Mr. Barlow all his present pocket-money, with a cheque for his next week's allowance, if he would not submit him to the practical test of Harry's new rack.

Harry. I trust, sir, that you will permit Master Tommy to try this instrument, as I am afraid that I have made neither the ropes nor the rollers sufficiently strong.

With some difficulty Mr. Barlow and Harry tied their young companion on the rack, the handle of which Master Harry, who could scarcely control his exuberant laughter, commenced to turn slowly, as though he were performing upon a barrel organ.

Harry's fears now proved to be well founded, for scarcely had he given the roller its second wrench, when the handle broke, the ropes gave way, and Tommy, springing frrom the machine, loudly announced his intention of at once running home and asking his parents, who were very fond of the study of history, to come down to Mr. Barlow's, and see, for themselves, Harry's clever workmanship.

Mr. Barlow pointed out to him, that ere he could visit his father and mother and return, Harry would have destroyed so imperfect and unsatisfactory a machine, and that he himself would scarcely be in a position to corroborate so astounding a statement as Tommy intended, according to his present purpose, to make concerning what he had pleased to term the torture chamber. Mr. Barlow showed him how useless such a course would be; how he would be credited by no one, but, on the contrary, would be deservedly scouted by all honest persons as a fabricator of false intelligence, a deceiver of his parents, and a reviler of his best friends.

Tommy was not insensible to these arguments, and, after a few minutes' deliberation, owned himself to have been entirely in the wrong, begging pardon both of his tutor, and of Harry, for the mischief which he might have caused by his impetuous desire of sharing his knowledge with his beloved kindred.

Mr. Barlow. I will now dictate an exercise, which you will be good enough to render into the French language as I proceed.

Mr. Barlow's French Exercise.

Can you swim in the counting-house?—No, I cannot swim in the counting-house.

Has the gardener's son gold ribands (des rubans d'or)?

Does the shoemaker intend to go to the ball?

Have you the fine gun and the big nose?— No, sir, my father has the fine gun, and I have the big nose.

Are you a Scotchman?—No, a Russian.

Is the Dutchman in the counting-house with the bad eggs and the fine gun?—Yes, he is.

The merchant is swimming with (avec) the gardener's son, but (mais) the Dutchman has the gun.

Translation of the above into French by Masters Harry and Tommy.

*Swimmezvous dans le magazine maison?—
Non moi ne swimmy pas dans le magazine
maison.
Avy le Gardinier's fils des rubans d'or—d'or
not? eh?
Intendy le soulier facteur to ally to the bal?
Avezvous le fuzee magnifique et le grand
Ney?
Non Mossoo mon père avy le fuzee magnifique
et moi avy le grand ney.
Etes-vous un Scossmossoo? Non un Russ-
mossoo.
Le Dootchmossoo isit-il dans le magazine
maison avec les œufs de rottong et le magnifique
fuzee?
Le merchand il swimmy avec le gardinier's
fils mais le Dootchman avy le fuzee.*

Mr. Barlow now expressed himself highly pleased with their progress in French, and as Tommy had copied Harry's exercise by looking over his shoulder, their revered tutor awarded to the latter the first prize, and to the former the second, the butler being called in to hold them both down in turn, in order to receive the reward of merit, which in Harry's case was conferred upon him with the cane, and in Tommy's with the apple-twig birch. After this, it being twelve o'clock, Mr. Barlow struck his gong, and dismissed the classes for an hour's recreation, previous to re-assembling at dinner.

Thus happily passed away the study-time at Mr. Barlow's.

CHAPTER XXIII.

APPROACH OF HOLIDAYS. MR. BARLOW AT BRIGHTON. TOMMY'S MYSTERIOUS CONDUCT.

HE Christmas holidays were now fast approaching, when honest Farmer Sandford had promised to keep the festive season, in true old English fashion, under his own roof. Tommy had been invited by Harry Sandford to spend a few days at Pyggedale Farm, where he would be hospitably entertained with such fare as, he said, an 'umble farm-house could offer to one of his wealth and position.

Farmer Sandford called on Mr. Merton at Tiffin House during Mr. Barlow's absence at the sea-side, where, it was rumoured, that he was paying honourable attentions to a Mrs. Simmons, a lady conspicuous no less by her irreproachable virtue, than by the vast wealth, of which she had become possessed, on the decease of the worthy Mr. Simmons, who had, unfortunately, fallen a victim to the treachery of the savages of Interior Africa, while engaged in negotiating the exchange of three beads, and a left-foot slipper, for a crock of gold, a war-horse, and three suits of African armour, complete. Such was the account of the fate of the ill-starred Mr. Simmons, whose stirring life and adventures had been published in the "Christian Midsummer Monthly Magazine," where he had been advertised for, during several months, under the heading of "Missing Missionaries." Satisfied at length of his decease, Mrs. Simmons gave herself up to grief, and took a house at Brighton for the winter season. Here she was to be seen every morning, in black robes of the deepest dye, though of the most elegant fashion, walking on the pier, and listening to the measured notes of the band, which seemed to affect her to tears as she looked out towards the horizon. Then she would, in an almost fainting state, allow herself to be conducted to the refreshment-room, where respectable elderly gentlemen—generally strangers to the place—were ready to assist her, with the utmost eagerness, to such restoratives as their politeness and tenderness could suggest.

It was on one of these occasions that Mr. Barlow—ever watchful to render himself of service to his fellow-creatures, encountered the unfortunate lady, whose sad history was now known to all the residents of that gay watering-place.

Nothing was wanting on the part of Mr. Barlow to render her recovery as perfect as possible; but, finding that, after using all the means in his power, she remained insensible to his efforts on her behalf, he, with great consideration, paid for the agreeable liquor, and had the afflicted widow conveyed to her residence in a bath-chair.

The next day the poor lady could not sufficiently evince her gratitude for all his labour and trouble, and expressed her most sincere wishes that their unforeseen meeting might be the commencement of so lasting a friendship as nothing but death could terminate.

Mr. Barlow, now, invariably spent his scant vacations either at Brighton or at some other watering-place, according to the requirements of the season, and the precarious health of the still ailing Mrs. Simmons. "I feel," said Mr. Barlow, one Sunday evening to her, as they walked on the pier while the band performed several airs of a sacred character from the Oratorio of *Balaam*, "I feel that you, my dear madam, are a holy charge to me; that to me is entrusted the care of interests far exceeding those which are the mere returns of niggardly investments."

At the word "niggardly" the poor lady's tears commenced afresh, and Mr. Barlow, fearful of having struck a chord which reminded her of the fate which her husband had met with at the

hands of the remorseless blacks, begged her to compose herself; "for," said he, "remember that this is Sunday night, and as neither the honest refreshment-room keepers are present, nor is their store available to us, weak human nature can have no relief except from the bottle,—I mean, my dear madam, the smelling-bottle,—with which, as I observe you have not provided yourself, I now bless the forethought which inspired me to bring it." So saying, he drew from his pocket an elegant glass vial, the lower part of which being encased in a cup formed of the silver of Germany, and unscrewing the top, he with ineffable grace and politeness handed it to Mrs. Simmons, who, after inhaling the refreshing fragrance of its contents, placed the mouth of the bottle to her lips, whence she did not remove it, until she felt she could do so without fear of incurring the danger of a relapse.

It was, then, during the absence of Mr. Barlow on a visit of moral consolation to Mrs. Simmons, that Farmer Sandford had a long conversation with Mr. Merton.

In homely but forcible language he inquired of Tommy's father whether, considering the position which his son would assuredly hold in the county, it were not better for him to become thoroughly acquainted with all such subjects as concerned the tillage of the soil and the social condition of the agriculturists, than to learn the very finest treatises in Greek or Latin, or to be parleyvooing in "thic theer frenchy nonsense, dang 'un, an' a curdling an' coombing his hair an' bowing and scrapin' like a dancin' measter? Whoy blesser 'art, oi'll be bound oi'll teach 'un morre to the porpoise in a fortnight, than arl thic theer old Barlow could du in a month, blarm'd if oi doan't."

Tommy, who had in the meantime been summoned by his father to hear Farmer Sandford's proposition, appeared very much abashed by this implied rebuke. He hung down his head in silence a considerable time: at length he faintly said, "Oh, sir! I have indeed acted very ill: I have rendered myself unworthy of the affection of my best friends, among whom I have the greatest pleasure in counting the honourable Mister Sandford and his excellent son. But do not, my dear father, do not, I pray, give me up entirely to Mr. Barlow, who,—but I will add no more. Permit me to remain at home, freed from all such cares as are entailed by study and the use of the globes, and see how I shall behave for the future. I know, sir, what faults to avoid, and should I ever be guilty of the same again, or should I ever repeat one single trick, practical joke, or conundrum, that I have already perpetrated, then, sir, I consent that you shall abandon me for ever. From this moment I am changed, in manners, in morals, in habiliments, and in demeanour. Farewell, my dear father, my dear mother, and honourable friend, for the present; it will not, perhaps, be many minutes before you hear, once more, from your ardent and sincere admirer, Tommy."

Thus saying he waved his hand, and silently stole out of the room, as if intent upon some extraordinary resolution.

CHAPTER XXIV.

SHOWING WHAT TOMMY MEANT BY IT. ALSO WHAT CAME OF IT, WHATEVER HE MEANT BY IT. HARRY NARRATES THE TWELFTH STORY.

His father, turning to Mr. Sandford, said "What can this 'ere portend? This boy his has wariable has a vethercock. Hevery blast virls 'im round an' round upon his centre, an' he won't not never fix in hany direckshun."

"You stick to what oi zay, Muster Merton," returned the honest farmer; "Let 'un coom oop t' farm wi' me an' my zun, an' you pay me quarterly in advance fur such an eddicayshun as'll do un good. I'll do 't fur half o' thic theer Barlow, and giv 'un 'ealth an' appiness bezide."

Mr. Merton considered for a few seconds, and remembering that his second instalment would soon be due to Mr. Barlow, he said, "I ham hindeed werry much hobliged for your hadwice; but you hair not perraps haware—"

"Law bless 'ee," interrupted the worthy farmer, "I knaw it arl. I knaw yer difficulty, zur, and be main glad, that I be, to zettle with thic Barlow for you. Let 'un carl on me;" and so saying he thumped his stout stick on the floor, and shook his head, with all the marks of genuine indignation, of which his rough nature was capable.

Tommy now entered the room, but with a remarkable change in his dress and manner. He had demolished the elegance of his curls, and had cut his own hair himself. He had also washed all the pomade out of it with soda and water. In order to show himself strictly economical, he had selected a pair of his father's pantaloons, which he had divested of all such ornamentation as stripes down the sides, and had cut them so as to suit his own length. On the same plan he had dealt with a frilled shirt of his father's, which he had reduced to the plainest pattern, and, in order to save his indulgent parent the expense of a tailor's bill for a jacket, he had, with marvellous ingenuity, contrived to bereave of its tails one of Mr. Merton's blue coats, from which also he had removed the velvet collar and the gilt buttons, so that, with some further abridgment at the cuffs, it now served him for an admirable jacket. Every article of his attire was plain and simple. Thus habited he appeared so totally changed from what he had been, that his mother, entering the room suddenly, burst into tears and threw her arms round her husband, whose feelings seemed for the moment to have utterly overcome him.

"Vot?" exclaimed Mr. Merton, "in the name of——"

"Wonder," suggested Mrs. Merton, who was still clinging to her husband, whom indeed, she nearly overpowered by the vehemence of her embraces.

"Vell—Vot—hin the name o' vunder ave the hinf——"

"Hinterestin," suggested his wife.

"Vell—'Ave the hinterestin young willin been a doin of vith my best Sunday——"

"'Ush!" murmured Mrs. Merton.

Farmer Sandford smiled, and seeing that Mr. Merton was by this time less agitated, looked towards Master Tommy for an explanation.

"Papa, Mamma, and the Honourable Mr. Sandford," answered Tommy, gravely, "I am now only what I ought always to have been. Had I been content with this dress before, I should not have been praised for my personal appearance, nor led away by vanity to join in the wild gaiety which I have witnessed around me. Had my sleeves always been a trifle too long for me, my little hands would not have been free to indulge in mischief, and had my continuations been troublesome at the ancles, and tight at the waist, I should not, perhaps, have stooped to meannesses which I now despise; nor, had my boots and shoes been such as you now behold," he was wearing his father's, which he had somewhat altered for his own convenience, "should I ever have walked in any paths but those of the most exalted virtue and propriety. From this time forth I shall cultivate nothing but reason, philosophy, and——"

"And farming," said Mr. Sandford, whereat Mr. Merton nodded affirmatively.

"Farmin' an' fillosofy both begin wi' a f," said Mr. Sandford, looking at Tommy, who appeared considerably astonished at the information which this interruption of the honest farmer's conveyed to him.

"I thought," continued Tommy, "that I should have been permitted to study at home, and that my adored and venerated mother would never again have allowed her son——"

"It's settled, Tommy," said Mrs. Merton, "as you goes back with Mr. Sandford, just to learn farmin' and stay the 'olidays with 'im, which 'll do you a deal o' good, has me an' your father bein' arks'd to London to go to parties and pantomines, don't want to be bothered with a boy 'anging on to our skirts. So, as your thinks is packed, you can go, and when you come back just be'ave, or you don't get no pity from me, I can tell you."

Tommy could scarcely conceal his emotion on hearing this address, whereupon Farmer Sandford, seeing that to prolong the interview might be painful to all present, hastily placed a cheque-book before Mr. Merton, a leaf of which the latter signed and handed over to Harry's father, expressing a hope that Tommy would henceforth imitate his papa's example and "turn over a new leaf;" and Farmer Sandford thereupon took

Tommy by the collar, roughly but heartily wished Mr. and Mrs. Merton good-day, and, with his young charge, quitted the apartment.

They now commenced setting out on foot, but Mr. Merton insisted upon sending them in his carriage with all his horses and a whole retinue of black servants, so that the good country people, seeing the approach of the grand equipage, flocked to the spot for miles round, under the impression that the Travelling Horse-riders, which was their favourite amusement in those parts, were about to pay them a visit. They were soon undeceived by Mr. Sandford, whom, in their disappointment they were for treating somewhat roughly, had not his farm labourers, fortunately, arrived on the spot, and laid about them with convincing energy. As it was, the horses took fright at a cracker which Master Harry, who was in the crowd, had thrown out in order to disperse the people, and ran with the vehicle headlong into a mill-stream. Master Tommy had contrived to climb down from the rumble where he had been sitting, and was running away, calling for help, in the direction of Mr. Merton's house, when Harry, who, after witnessing his father's misfortune, had retired from the concourse in order to indulge his merriment, suddenly came up with Tommy, whom he seized round the waist, protesting he was so glad to see him again, that nothing should ever induce him any more to part with his amiable young friend.

"Your conduct, my dear Harry," said Tommy, "reminds me of *Crysos*——"

"——*And the Perverse Basket Maker,*" said Harry, "which I have not only heard, but was myself the first to narrate to you. But as we are now at Pyggedale Farm, we will have our milk and porridge first, and afterwards, as you are our guest, you shall narrate to our family circle, as none of them have heard it, the story of *Agesiläus and the Elastic Nobleman.*"

After their simple meal, which consisted of jam and shrimps, Farmer Sandford, who had partaken heartily of veal pie, stout, bacon, coffee, and eggs, lighted his pipe, and beckoning the two boys to do the same, while Mary the maid brought in a bowl of steaming punch and some glasses, Tommy, according to the previous arrangement, commenced the story, to which his companions, including the entire Sandford family, of whom we have not yet spoken, listened with prodigious interest.

CHAPTER XXV.

Story the Twelfth.

Agesiläus and the Elastic Nobleman.

AGESILÄUS, on returning victoriously to the throne of his ancestors, determined to choose as his prime minister some man of undoubted honour, integrity, and virtue, whose principles should be exactly in accordance with those which he himself had, from his earliest infancy, professed.

Such an one he considered he had found in Chronon, who was of so pliant a disposition that he could double himself up in a ball, stand on his head with his left leg round his neck, and

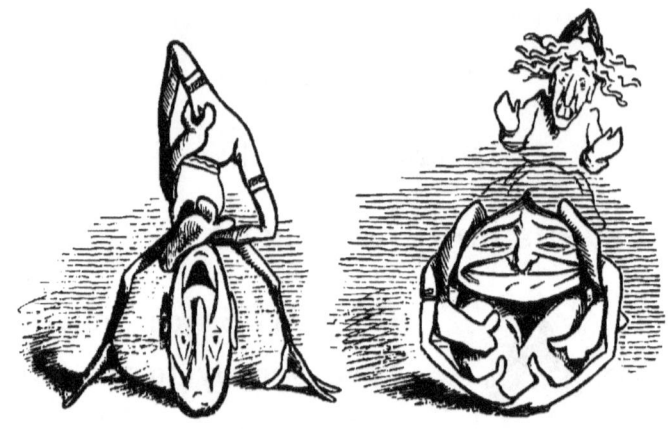

his right foot in his trowser pocket; and, indeed, could render himself so generally agreeable, that he was beloved not only by all who knew him, but by everyone who had only heard of him.

The garden of this nobleman, for such was the rank of Chronon, was planted with richly flowering india-rubber trees, spring radishes, spring cabbage, all growing in spring beds, which were moistened by springs of fresh water. In short, there was nothing in the garden, or in the house, but partook of the character of its master.

Agesiläus now frequently consulted Chronon on such emergencies as arose either in his home or in the state.

"I will give you," he said to Chronon one day, "two million piastres if you will be my Chief Chamberlain.'"

Chronon sprang from his seat, and, at a single bound, jumped at the offer. In this new capacity he was of the utmost service to Agesiläus. It is true he made many enemies, who attempted, under cover of false friendship, to seduce him from the paths of honesty. "No," answered the virtuous Chronon, "I feel that my gratitude to Agesiläus can never know suf-  ficient bounds." Here he kicked out right and left, and sent the conspirators flying in all directions; then he tucked both his legs under his arms, and walked on his hands into the house. Agesiläus could not but admire such admirable conduct on the part of his minister, and foreseeing that his popularity would in course of time render him the greatest possible favourite with the people, he privately commanded his assassination.

Nor, perhaps, was this the only reason for the monarch's wish to be rid of his elastic minister, as it so happened that at this time there was engaged in a menial capacity, at the Court, a young and lovely maiden, who was called by all Cancanina; and, indeed, this was her real name.

Agesiläus, inflamed with a passion which was as unreasonable as it was impolitic, determined to take the earliest opportunity of declaring his true sentiments. Having craftily given all the ministers and officers of the Court permission to make an excursion into the neighbouring country; and having granted, unasked, a holiday to all his domestics, with the exception of Cancanina, whom he deputed to remain at home and attend the kitchen of the palace, he gave his hair an additional curl, and, arrayed in his most splendid robes, quietly descended the back-stairs which led to the culinary department of his royal residence.

He felt his heart palpitating with the most violent emotion as he entered the pantry. But what was his consternation at hearing sounds of merriment proceeding from the kitchen. He had but sufficient time to step adroitly into a capacious linen press, when through the crevices  of the cupboard door, which he had carefully closed after him, he saw Chronon and Cancanina enter together, laughing and dancing, the latter having in her hand a sieve, which she was treating as though it were a tambourine, while her companion was pretending to perform several measures of a voluptuous character on the burnished warming-pan which he handled like a guitar.

"What did they sing?" asked Harry.

"I will tell you," answered Tommy, and forthwith recited the following charming ballad :—

"I LOVE MY LOVE."

I love my love in the morning,
    And in the afternoon;
I love my love in the dawning,
    When chasing of the coon.
I love my love,
        With my rum-ti-tum,
And with my tweedle-dee,
    Excuse my globe,
        My love,
        My dove,
But say that you love me.

"Let's have a coalbox to it," exclaimed honest Farmer Sandford heartily, meaning by "coalbox" a chorus, and immediately began shouting lustily, in which he was joined by his two young friends, his wife, his daughters, his grandmother, and the rest of the Sandford family:—

> Excoose my globe,
> My love,
> My dove,
> An' say as you love me.

After the company had, with much moderation, refreshed themselves, Tommy resumed his solo with so much spirit, and with so clear and ringing a voice, that the dogs in the yard began howling, and not only the animals of the farm, but the ploughboys also who slept out, were roused from their first slumber, and coming from their various places of repose, gathered about the windows and doors, in order to enjoy the harmony.

"Second verse," said Tommy.

"Hear, hear!" cried Farmer Sandford and all the family, including Farmer Sandford's grandmother, who was sitting up late, for this night only; a proceeding which, she said, would probably kill her; but in which, however, she was encouraged by her grandson, who, as the sole heir to her fortune, was warmly attached to the old lady.

SECOND VERSE.

I love my love in the ev=en=in',
And in the night time too;
I'll love my love when we've an inn
The sign of the Baldfaced Coo.

Chorus.

I love my love
With my rum=ti=tum,
And with my tweedle=dee,
Excuse my glove,
My love,
My dove,
And say that you love me.

After the repetition of the chorus, Tommy insisted upon singing all he could recollect of the song.

I love my love in the twilight,
　　I love her in the sheen,
　　I'd love my love on a skylight,
　　Or on the village green.

Chorus.　　I love my love with my, &c.

　　I love my love in the day-time,
　　I love her when I dine;
　　I love my love in the Maytime,
　　And here's to the good Rhine wine!

Chorus.　　I love my love with my, &c.

Another bowl of punch, as hot as it was strong, having been brewed by the honest farmer, Master Tommy proceeded with his story of the Elastic Nobleman.

Agesiläus was now compelled to witness a scene which would have caused him to shake with rage and jealousy, had his hiding place admitted the indulgence of these emotions. Chronon conducted himself on no ordinary rules of courtship, and in Cancanina, it was evident he had found a warm sympathiser and ardent admirer. Instead of embracing her, or going down on his knees to her, as rapturous lovers usually do under the circumstances, he, while declaring his deep affection for her, threw first one leg, then another,

over her head, dancing away from, and then up to her, then throwing himself on to his hands, with his feet in the air, with such graceful and expressive gestures, that there was not one attitude, or one movement, but had its own peculiar meaning, and which did not go, at once, and directly, to the maiden's heart. She on her part, was in no way behindhand in her demonstrations of reciprocal attachment; and at last, on Chronon pulling from his pocket an enormous hourglass, and pointing to the time marked on it, she gave one bound and a twirl, and taking his hand, threw herself into an elegant position, with one hand and one foot stretched out as though she were either swimming or flying, while

the toe of her right foot just touched the floor, serving as a pivot for her to be turned round upon by her devoted admirer. Then she threw herself, as though fainting, right across him, so as to be supported by his left arm, while with his right hand he tickled the tip of her nose with a strawberry.

Then resuming their song, they danced across the room, and out at the door, with so much energy, and so great contentment shown on their beaming faces, that Agesiläus perceived that they were gone to be married, and that *his* suit could never prosper with the fair Cancanina.

He now meditated revenge, and, as I have said, gave orders for Chronon's assassination.

Ten of his boldest bravoes waylaid Chronon, on the following afternoon, as he was returning, unarmed, from the bath.

Vain were their attempts to wound the Elastic Nobleman, who, now on their shoulders, now under their legs, now buffeting this one, now jumping down from the top of a tree and crushing another, eluded all their efforts ; and, having possessed himself of a swinging steel life-preserver with spikes to it, much used in those days, he laid about him with so good a will, that the ten villains within as many minutes were lying on the road, the victims of their own misplaced confidence.

After this Agesiläus showed himself most amicably disposed towards Chronon, and even went so far as to ask him to encounter him in the public games, which were forthwith to take place. To be the antagonist of so proud a monarch was no slight honour, and Chronon could not choose but avail himself of the royal favour. Agesiläus now tried to accomplish by deceit, what he could not compass by fair and open dealing. When they were shaking hands, in the arena, previous to the struggle, Agesiläus attempted to stab the brave Chronon, who, fortunately for himself, being as quick with his legs as with his arms, dealt the crafty monarch so severe a blow on the side of his head with his left foot, that it was some time before he could sufficiently recover himself in

order to confront his antagonist. After giving his word of honour to have recourse to no farther wiles, it might have been expected that Agesiläus would have been contented to rely upon his skill in the use of the weapons with which he had been provided. But, alas, for human nature, the rage of Agesiläus against his former favourite was uncontrollable, and with all the madness of inveterate hate, rushing upon Chronon when his back was turned, and he was engaged in tying his sandal, he aimed a javelin at him. Chronon was calm as he was brave; he saw the necessity of defending his own life against the attacks of a perfidious friend, and with an agile spring turned three complete somersaults backwards, during which he finished tying his sandal, and alighting behind the incensed Agesiläus, dealt him so sound a cuff, with the flat sole of his right foot, as sent the ill-fated monarch flying up to the highest row of the back seats of spectators. On being brought down again from this elevation, Agesiläus, who had by this time lost most of the prestige which his subjects had been accustomed to attach to his name, detected some sounds among the occupants of the circle which nothing but the most abject flattery, or intense personal vanity, could have construed into expressions of admiration and applause. Agesiläus muttered fearful imprecations against his favourite minister, but controlling himself to the utmost, approached him. As they were walking towards one another with uplifted weapons, Agesiläus, being within a sword's thrust of his opponent, suddenly pointed upwards, directing his attention to something which the crafty monarch pretended to see in the sky. The unsuspicious Chronon turned his gaze towards the spot indicated, when, immediately, Agesiläus, nerving himself for the effort, made one step forward, and would have driven his weapon through his antagonist's body, had not Chronon's skin, by long use and practice, been of so tough and elastic a material that it turned the edge of the sword, which was, thenceforth, rendered useless. Agesiläus at once threw himself upon him, and they struggled for a time with all the efforts which disappointed rage could inspire on the one side, and virtuous indignation on the other. Agesiläus griped his adversary with such tenacity, that though Chronon turned somersaults, stood on his head, walked on his hands, and rolled over and over, he could not free himself from his grasp. At length the coolness, or rather, as it will be seen, the heat, of Chronon prevailed over the blind fury of Agesiläus, for the temperature of Chronon's body reached such a height that he seemed to be made entirely of india-rubber. Taking advantage of this extraordinary quality, he fell upon Agesiläus and began rubbing him out. In a few seconds Agesiläus would have been entirely obliterated, had he not owned himself vanquished, and begged for mercy.

"I will never hurt thee," replied the noble and generous Chronon, "but in my own just defence. Live, Agesiläus, to make a better use of life, and to have juster ideas of honour."

So saying, he assisted him to arise, and Agesiläus was so struck by the magnanimity of his minister that he determined, on the first opportunity, to impeach and behead him for high treason, an opportunity which, however, never offered itself, as Chronon, after consulting his wife, determined upon poisoning the ungrateful monarch. This he contrived to do the next morning, and thus, having ascended the throne, he, finding that he had a scruple of conscience concerning his wife's position, ordered Caucanina to be drowned.

𝔖𝔬 𝔰𝔥𝔢 𝔴𝔞𝔰 𝔡𝔯𝔬𝔴𝔫𝔢𝔡,
𝔄𝔫𝔡 𝔥𝔢 𝔴𝔞𝔰 𝔠𝔯𝔬𝔴𝔫𝔢𝔡,

amid the joyful plaudits of the people, from whom he received the title of Elastikos the First, and lived happily ever afterwards.

CHAPTER XXVI.

CONTINUATION OF THE EVENING AT FARMER SANDFORD'S.

HE Sandfords thanked Master Tommy for his narrative, which they all said was the best, the gracefullest, the most beautifullest and affectingest story they had ever heard; and Angelina Sandford, the elder, who was seventeen years old, and just returned from school, whispered to her mother, that, "for her part, she had often heard of such a perfect being as Master

Merton, but had never yet seen one, and that she was desperately enamoured of him," a confession which caused Tommy to pass his hand over his hair, which he now regretted having cropped so closely, and to take another tumbler of the generous punch which Miss Jemima, the younger Miss Sandford, blushingly poured out for him.

Farmer Sandford now volunteered a song. His daughters, and indeed the whole family, expressed themselves overjoyed at the announcement, as they had hoped never to have heard him sing again, and had trusted that this evening would have proved no exception to the rule. They even went so far as to beg him to postpone so great a treat until some future time, but the honest farmer was unwilling to deprive them of any gratification, and having cleared his throat with a jorum, thus commenced, singing with so many trills, inflections of voice, and variations of tune as were calculated to delight any audience that might be passionately fond of a florid style of music :

"MY LOVE IS LIKE."

My lobe be loike the red, red roze,
Arl in the marnin' earr=lee;
She 'abe a zart o' booteous noze,
An' teeth az be zo pearr=lee.

(*Singing very high and straining his voice.*)

My lobe be loike the water=lily trew,
She be zo pink and pratty,
And loike the dabby=down=dillee tu,
When she be drezed zo natty.

(*Coming down again.*)

My lobe be loike the olly=ock,
Zo gentle an' zo pewer;
My lobe be loike the Mizzuz Pollock,
Which be a ge=ra=ni=um flewer.

Here the chorus, was warmly demanded by Farmer Sandford, and responded to by the audience with equal fervour. After this, they knocked the table and applauded vehemently, thinking that it was the last verse, an impression which was immediately dispelled by Farmer Sandford bowing to them and proceeding with his ballad.

> My love be loike the zgarlet rooner,
> She be zo white and modest;
> My love be loike zome flewer [I <u>dun</u> kna'
> Its name] when she be boddic'd.
>
> My love be loike the dandy=lion ble=ew,
> Loike daizies on a bough;
> An' zo, friends arl, I drink to yew,
> An' to the Barley Mow.

As there could by no possibility be any mistake as to this being the last verse, it was received with rapturous applause, and it being known to everyone present that he was unacquainted with any other song, the party proceeded to surrender themselves to unalloyed enjoyment.

Neither Angelina, nor Jemima, could make enough of their guest, and Farmer Sandford viewed with undisguised delight the attachment which was evidently springing up between little Tommy Merton and one of his daughters; but which was the favoured object of his choice, neither Mr. nor Mrs. Sandford could, as yet, be perfectly certain.

As for Harry, he amused himself by tickling his great-grandmother's ear with a straw, which

sensation she attributed to a blue-bottle that had

outlived the summer season, and occasionally emptying the old lady's glass when her attention was directed towards another quarter. The hours now flew swiftly by while they indulged in their innocent and homely mirth, and when one o'clock struck, Farmer Sandford gravely arose from his chair; and as they were now pretty far advanced in a state of intoxication, the whole family retired to bed.

Thus ended Tommy's first evening under the roof of the hospitable Farmer Sandford.

CHAPTER XXVII.

MASTER TOMMY MERTON'S CONTINUED RESIDENCE IN THE BOSOM OF THE SANDFORD FAMILY. MR. BARLOW'S ASTONISHING RECEPTION.

HE next morning Tommy, who had now determined to adopt the early hours to which the honest and healthy country people, by whom he was surrounded, had long since accustomed themselves, rose punctually at eleven, and speedily proceeded to dress himself with his newly-attained simplicity. He now descended to the farm-parlour. This apartment was modestly furnished with profile portraits, in black, of Mr. and Mrs.

Sandford, as they had appeared years ago on the Brighton pier, a little shell house four inches high, wherein dwelt an eccentric lady and gentleman, whose prognostications as to the weather were considered infallible, some curiously coloured china ornaments, a picture in a black frame of Jezebel, in a red dress, being thrown out of window, a teakettle-holder, worked by Mrs. Sandford before her marriage, a variegated tea-board, a silver teapot, and many other works of art, besides the ordinary chairs and tables, which were of a plain but serviceable pattern and of strong workmanship. The family were not yet down when Tommy entered the room; but a few minutes after he had commenced to spread some jam upon a piece of bread, which he had cut for himself, Miss Angelina appeared, and welcomed him with the sweetest grace imaginable.

Harry's mother, who presided over the urn and teapot, was a comely dame of about forty years of age, and Harry's great-grandmother, who assisted at the buttered toast, was a plain, venerable, old lady of about seventy-six, but so hale and upright that there was in her appearance all the promise of her getting beyond the century.

The family, one and all, were most attentive to her, they gave her everything they could possibly think of to eat and drink, and, in their eagerness to help her, mixed tea and coffee with beer, bacon with strawberry jam, and invariably selected for her the choice morsels of the bread in which the blackbeetles had been baked. In the fruit season, so great was their anxiety that she should have the first of everything, that nothing was too unripe, nothing too early, nothing too green for their beloved great-grandmother. Did she feel faint and complain of heat, they at once rushed to place her chair in a thorough draught; did she complain of cold, they shut her into her warm and comfortable room, closed the windows, and lighted a brazier of charcoal in the middle of the apartment. With all this care and attention, arising out of the respect due to old age, Mrs. Sandford had arrived at her present time of life, and seemed to defy the infirmities which usually accompany so advanced a period of existence. She possessed about five hundred pounds a year of her own, and though her grandson had every reason to suppose that he would be her sole heir, yet he had owned to his wife that he still felt some little uncertainty as to the nature of the will, which she had perhaps never made, or if she had, it was what he most certainly had never yet seen.

Angelina, aged seventeen, and Jemima, aged fifteen, were Harry's two sisters, and were modest fresh-looking girls, whose pink and white complexions, brilliant eyes, jet-black eyebrows and lashes, golden hair, high-heeled boots, and dresses of all the colours of the rainbow, would have had their effect upon hearts far less impressionable than that of Master Tommy Merton. These young ladies, and indeed the entire family, Master Tommy treated with so much politeness, cordiality, and attention, that all the company were delighted with him. So easy it is for those who possess rank and fortune to gain the goodwill of their fellow-creatures. Tommy now placed himself between Angelina and Jemima, who professed themselves prodigiously honoured by the attentions of so gallant a young gentleman, and they in their turn lost no opportunity of helping him to sugar, honey, eggs, and a delicious compound made out of the liver of the goose, preserved with a few roots buried in it, and some lard spread over it, of which simple food Master Tommy formed so high an opinion, that he vowed he far preferred it to all the mutton and beef he had ever tasted at his father's table.

Harry dutifully waited upon his great-grandmother, to whom he took care to give scalding-hot tea without any sugar in it, and for whom he thoughtfully cut off all the choice corner bits of the outside crust of the loaf, which, five times in succession, fetched old Mrs. Sandford's handsome false teeth out of her head. These he was doing his best to search for under the table, when Tommy suddenly cried out that some dog had bitten his calf, whereupon the two young ladies dragged their brother from his concealment, and set upon him with so good a will, that Farmer Sandford was obliged to rescue him from their hands; but not before he had received such marks of the encounter as would last him for some considerable time. His father now read him a severe lecture on the crime of inhospitality, and threatened to inflict a far worse punishment upon him than what he had already received, did he not that instant go down upon his knees, " and," as Mrs.

Sandford added, with much feeling, "beg that little cherub's pardon who had come to this our 'umble 'ome on an angel's visit, which is, indeed, few and far between."

Harry now complied with his father's request; and Tommy, raising him in his arms, owned he had never felt for any one single person half so much esteem and affection as he did for the whole Sandford family at that moment. He now requested to be allowed to salute Mrs. Sandford and the two young ladies, who responded with an ardour which admitted no doubt of their sincerity. In the afternoon, when Miss Angelina and Jemima had gone with their mother, in their hats, feathers, and riding-habits, to pay a few calls, and while Farmer Sandford, whip in hand, was watching Harry ploughing in the field, Tommy, complaining of a headache, lay down in his own room. Here old Mrs. Sandford looked in, and beckoned him to follow her. She was sure, she said, that Master Tommy required some amusement; and as he had no sisters of his own, she would have great pleasure in showing him her great-granddaughters' wardrobes, and the charming appointments of their room. Tommy, being of a yielding disposition, and unwilling to pain even the most helpless, accompanied the old lady to the room which was set apart for the use of the young ladies, of whose beauty, specially of Miss Angelina's, he felt it were impossible any longer to conceal his admiration.

Old Mrs. Sandford, possessing a master key, as it seemed, of all the drawers, now proceeded to show him bunches of light hair similar to that worn by her great-granddaughters. These she instructed Tommy how to fix and remove. He was now intensely interested at being shown several small paint-brushes, a little box of Indian ink, some white paste labelled "Blondine," and a small white china pot of a flower-pot shape, with a brilliant colour spread out on the top, which the venerable lady informed him was called "rouge," and that without all these things the young ladies would have neither complexion nor beauty.

Tommy replied that until then he had thought it was only savages who painted their faces, and that then it was to intimidate the foe.

"You are indeed right," returned old Mrs. Sandford; "but in this country the ladies do it in order to attract the unwary, who only find out too late that they have got a doll, when they thought to have married a woman. They think they'll have my money, but——"

At this instant the sound of footsteps on the gravel path warned them that, for the present, their instructive amusement must come to an end, not however before Tommy, whose generous nature could not tolerate deception, no matter in how beautiful a shape it might present itself, had cut with a pair of scissors the false hair to half its length, taken away with him all the paint-boxes, rouge-pots, and other similar articles on which he could lay his hands, and had carefully secreted them in his own box. That evening, and the next day, the young ladies pleaded indisposition, and indeed there is no knowing how long their malady might have continued, had not Farmer Sandford, who would not hear of such, as he termed it, uncourteous conduct towards their guest, insisted upon their coming down to tea, and being up for breakfast.

Both Mr. and Mrs. Sandford were now astonished beyond measure at the ravages which two days' illness had made on their daughters' countenances. Instead of the brilliant complexion of a week ago, they were now of one uniform sallow tint; they showed no signs of eyebrows, except a few straggling hairs; and their eyelashes were of a dirt-white tinge. As for their hair they really appeared to have none left, where once there had been a profusion.

"Heavens, children! what *is* the matter?" exclaimed their mother, in accents of the deepest alarm.

"Dang un!" cried Farmer Sandford, who was no less surprised than his good wife, "dang un!

if they bean't been moultin' loike t' ould fowls; and," he presently added, finding that instead

of offering any explanation, they would only sit in silence, until at length they burst into a flood of tears, "dang'd if they ain't got the doomb-madness!"

In the meantime no one seemed to be so well and thriving on the farm as Master Tommy, whose cheeks were blooming brighter and brighter every day, while his eyebrows and lashes were assuming that rich jet colour which is a sign of genuine health; in short, whenever Tommy

went among the labourers, all the people in the place stood mute with admiration at the condescension of a young gentleman who was as liberal as he was rich, and was as gifted as he was beautiful. The additional exercise he used, improved his health and strength, and added so considerably to his appetite and growth, that Farmer Sandford, who perceived with regret the continued indisposition of his daughters, vowed that little Tommy exceeded all the boys he had ever known; and forthwith sent so glowing an account of him to his father, that Mr. Merton at once replied that he was beyond measure gratified at learning the state of his son's health and the extent of his appetite, but that as a bargain was a bargain, he should certainly not receive him back until the appointed time after Christmas, nor would he send one sixpence more than the stipulated sum for Master Tommy's weekly maintenance.

Tommy now thoroughly enjoyed his change of life, and soon found, from his own experience, that there is nothing which so tends to elevate the mind, as to have more than sufficient means to supply your own wants, and to live among those who are of an inferior class to your own.

Mr. Barlow, who had returned from Brighton

in a chastened spirit, called several times on
Mr. Merton, whom he was never able to find at
home. He now turned his attention towards little
Tommy, whom he visited frequently at Farmer
Sandford's, but was unable to see him; and, on
account of old Grumpy, and the other savage dogs,
which roamed loose about the premises, he could
not enter either the garden, or the house itself.

One day it so happened that Farmer Sandford,
having taken all his dogs out shooting, Mr.
Barlow, cautiously approaching the farmhouse,
caught a glimpse of Tommy at the second-floor
window.

"You are now," shouted Mr. Barlow, "beginning to practise those virtues which have rendered the great men of other times so justly
famous."

Here old Mrs. Sandford, who was an enthusiastic admirer of all open-air preaching, appeared
at the front door, and begged Mr. Barlow to
continue his beautiful discourse, of which she
should, she said, be sorry to lose one single word.

Nay, more, if he would step in and partake of a dish of tea, she would prepare it for him with her own hands.

Mr. Barlow could not resist so favourable an opportunity, and having refreshed himself with the simple beverage, of which Tommy also was pleased to partake, his beloved tutor thus continued : "It is not by sloth, no, nor finery, no, nor by the mean indulgence of our appetites,"— here old Mrs. Sandford sighed deeply, and handed him the buttered toast, which he, to whom a sufficiency was enough, put aside with a graceful motion of his hand—"no, not by these, that greatness of character, or even reputation, is to be acquired. He that would excel others in virtue, in the arts, in the sciences, in all knowledge, must first excel them in temperance "— here old Mrs. Sandford emptied the teapot and smoothed her apron — " in application and daily perseverance. You cannot imagine, my dear madam "—here the old lady closed her eyes and nodded—" nor you, my beloved pupil, that men fit to command an army, or to give laws to a state, or to excel in the pulpit"— another sigh from old Mrs. Sandford—" were ever formed by an idle and effeminate education. No, my dear madam, when the people, oppressed by their enemies, were looking out for a leader, where did they seek for this extraordinary man?"

"Give it up," said Tommy, much interested.

"I will tell you," replied Mr. Barlow. "Was it at banquets? No!"—here the maid answered the bell to take away the tea-things—"Was it in splendid palaces? No!"—("Very true," murmured old Mrs. Sandford.)—"Was it amongst the gay, the elegant, or the dissipated? No! a thousand times No!! They turned their steps towards a lowly cottage, they entered a farmhouse like this, and there they found a Cincinnatus like him"—here Mr. Barlow, who had risen from his seat, pointed to Farmer Sandford, who at that moment appeared at the door, having just returned from a blank day's shooting.

"What's that?" exclaimed the honest farmer, whose knowledge of history was not of much service to him on the present occasion, "What's that? Looky here, oi bean't no more a zinner than yourself, you danged old humbug; and oi tell 'ee what 'tis," he went on, thumping the table heavily with his fist, "oi wunna zee my guests put upon, be he who they may as tries it on, zo oi tell 'ee. Now then!"

"You are wrong, Farmer Sandford," commenced Mr. Barlow.

"Be oi? Well, oi'll be the right zide o' you presently zumhow, you cantin', sneakin', hipper-critteral old warmint you! Get out!"

"Mr. Sandford," said Mr. Barlow, who was now standing by the door, scarcely able, as he subsequently remarked, to trust his ears, "what would all the greatest men in England, nay, in this county, say were they to hear you, in not the most elegant or respectful language, requesting me to leave your house, to——."

"Get out," shouted Farmer Sandford, seizing

his gun ; "or az oi bain't shot nothing arl day, dang if oi doan't go in for a warmint like you."

Mr. Barlow retired briskly from the room, but addressing his young friends and Mr. Sandford from the outside of the window, he inquired of them : "Tell me, then, my young friends, would the ancient Romans, would the rugged Spartans, would the accomplished Greek——"

Here Harry, who, unobserved by the others, had been heating the kitchen poker, suddenly ran out and pursued Mr. Barlow, who fled with considerable alacrity towards the high road, where, on observing that the poker had once more resumed its accustomed appearance, he demanded of his two pupils, whether "they would accompany him, their beloved tutor, to his home, where all would be forgiven, or not ?"

Tommy replied to this invitation by thanking him generally for nothing in particular, and declared his resolution of staying with his friends until his father should again be ready to receive him at his own home ; after which he should, he trusted, no longer require a private tutor, who, after all, could teach him very little that he did not already know.

Mr. Barlow professed to approve of Tommy's design, and observed that the present circumstances forcibly reminded him of the story of the *Laplander and the Agreeable Peacock*, which, as none of them had heard it, he would now———. But at this moment the appearance of Mr. Sandford diverted his attention, and informing the worthy farmer that he should not in a hurry forget his hospitable treatment, which he might be sure he would take the earliest opportunity of repaying, he bowed to the assembled company, and promising the old lady that he would call in and tell her some other day the story which had just been interrupted, he gracefully took his leave and departed.

CHAPTER XXVIII.

OF CHRISTMAS-DAY AT FARMER SANDFORD'S. HOW IT WAS SPENT. EXCITING EVENT. END.

CHRISTMAS-DAY arrived at last, and a large party had assembled around Farmer Sandford's hospitable board, which on this occasion had been amply provided from Mr. Merton's larder.

Mistletoe was in every nook, and hanging from every possible place. Red noses vied with the colour of the berries, for it was a marvellously cold Christmas, and Farmer Sandford had made all his labourers bring into the house every stump and stick on which they could lay hands.

The Farmer himself took the head of the table, with a boar's head under his nose, which they all said was exactly like Mr. Barlow; and Mr. Barlow, who, on such an occasion, was received with every token of affection, professed himself mightily amused with the notion, saying, that at first he had taken the dish to be a donkey's head, in which case the likeness would have been rather that of Farmer Sandford than of himself, a jest whereat Mr. Sandford's grandmother laughed until she nearly swallowed her false teeth.

Turkeys, geese, mince pies, and puddings met the eye on every sideboard. There was port wine and sherry wine, negus and gin, whiskey and brandy, and, finally, an enormous plum pudding, which Tommy and Harry had assisted in stirring, placed in a lake of blue fire, on seeing which everyone cried "Oh!" as people do after a magnificent firework; and all the guests who had judiciously left one little interior corner still unfilled, smacked their lips, and evinced their lively approval of the course which they were about to take.

After dinner more fun began. The young ladies (who had now completely recovered their good looks, and entertained, too, a deep and lasting regard for Master Merton), pulled crackers with their brother and his young friend; and Harry found various means of nearly frightening his great-grandmother into fits, for besides the ordinary crackers, which would have been enough of themselves to upset the strongest nerves, there were wrapped up in the larger ones hideous masks, which he put on suddenly, and said "Bo!" in the old lady's ear. She had a fit about nine o'clock, and Harry, who could not see her suffering and remain unmoved, went into the passage and roared with laughter. When she recovered, which she did through Mr. Barlow's prompt attention with a snuff-box, the mistletoe game com-

s

menced, and everybody kissed everybody else, Mr. Barlow insisting upon embracing the old lady with the most profound and respectful courtesy. This attention on his part to old Mrs. Sandford was far from being welcome to Mrs. Simmons, who, happening to be in the neighbourhood, was one of the party that evening, and who, Farmer Sandford's wife considered, engrossed by far too much of the gentlemen's attention generally. But Mr. Merton had presented Mrs. Sandford, with a gold bracelet from the Lowther Arcade, and the two young ladies with pearl earrings, worth at least two shillings the set, and so she was determined that nothing on her part should disturb the harmony of the evening.

Mrs. Simmons indeed took Mr. Barlow to task in a corner, where, however, by producing the magic mistletoe, and initiating her into the Druidical rite, he soon restored her to her usual good temper, which had hardly once been ruffled since the news of her husband's decease.

"Words," said Mr. Merton, "hair hinsufficient to return the faviours has you've conferred on me and mine, Mister Sandford. So 'ere's your 'ealth and 'appiness, and many of 'em."

The toast was drunk with immense applause, and Farmer Sandford then replied.

He said. "Oi bean't much given to speechifyin' loike, but oi'll wrostle, an' tossel, wi' any lad o' my own zize and weight, an' I'll kiss the lasses under thic there mizzletoe with any man alive, or wumman neither. There bain't a better boy than my zun, Arry, ere, zave and 'zept his yoong friend Master Tommy Merton (*cheers for every-one and three times three*) as oi be proud to shake by the 'and, an' carl my frand. (*Immense applause.*) Oi du luke arn thic young gentleman as my flesh and blood, darned if oi doan't, for aren't he goin' to marry one o' my darters, zure? (*Cheers from Harry.*) That's zartain. An' if ee be a gentleman, an' cooms o' gentle stock, he bain't loikely to forego his wurd of *h*onour given to me by 'im *as* a gentleman (*hear, hear from*

Mrs. Sandford, Harry, and his two sisters), an' if he did go for to withdraw it, what follers? why zure and zartain there 'ud be work for t' laryers, joodges and 'zizes, and arl the rest of 'un, and a breach o' promise case for five thousand five 'underd pounds—fur oi've consulted a solizitur an it, an' he du zay zo—an' that's gosple trew as zure as my name's Jonathan Zandford. And zo I du drink tu Mr. Merton, and Mrs. Merton, Master Tommy, an' arl your jally good healths."

Tremendous applause succeeded Mr. Sandford's speech, after which Tommy rose to reply. He said that he experienced sentiments of the most heartfelt gratitude for the kind and handsome manner in which his excellent friend and benefactor had alluded to him and his parents. As to his impending marriage, Mister Sandford had indeed spoken truly, as he felt, that, as he could not be long without his dear friend Harry, so there was but one way to bind him to him for ever, and that was by marrying his eldest sister,

Angelina Sandford, who, he trusted would wait for him until he had arrived at an age when he would be in some sort worthy of so admirable a young lady. It was not his fault that he was now but twelve years old, nor hers, that she was close upon nineteen, "but Mr. Sandford," he continued, turning towards the farmer, who was deeply affected by his simple eloquence, " you have taught me that to wait is better than to want; that possession does not bring happiness; that the joys of wedlock are less real than ideal; while to Mr. Barlow I owe the maxims, that it is better to be great than amiable, and more noble to be splendidly vicious than to be unostentatiously virtuous. Ladies and gentlemen, I beg to propose the health of Mr. Barlow, coupled with that of Mrs. Simmons, who, if report speaks truly, will soon render a worthy and venerated man indefinably happy."

This toast was received enthusiastically; and "They are jolly good fellows" was musically given by Harry.

Mr. Barlow had scarcely risen from his seat and taken the lady, whose name had been coupled with his, by the hand, ere a startling rap was heard at the door, and a dairy-maid, entering, announced that a coloured gentleman, having lost his way in the snow, craved admission. The permission being accorded, Tommy and Harry had little trouble in recognising the black man who had so courageously engaged the bull, and had on that occasion announced himself as Mister Johnson.

"The very thing!" cried Harry; "he's brought his banjo, and we can have a dance."

The hospitable farmer at once ordered the supper to be cleared, in which indeed the black, who had not eaten anything since that morning, was prodigiously willing to assist; and when he had stuffed a fowl and some sausages into his pocket, and had satisfied the cravings of his appetite with blanc-mange and negus, he was called upon to perform Sir Roger de Coverley on the banjo, which he at once proceeded to execute.

Mr. Barlow now selected Mrs. Simmons for his partner, whom the poor black no sooner perceived than he uttered a loud exclamation of astonishment, and cried out—

"Golly! Niggar! It am my Eleanora!!" At the mention of this name, Mrs. Simmons gave a piercing scream, and would have fallen, but for Mr. Barlow, who supported her. When she had recovered her senses, the black man, who, in the meantime, having dashed at a napkin and a water-jug, had entirely cleansed his face from all traces of his recent Ethiopian colour, stood before her.

"Eleanora!" he cried.

In a moment she had recognised him, and springing towards him, fell on his neck, exclaiming—

"Alexander! Richard!! Simmons!!!"

Then, in a sudden transport of joy, and without consideration of circumstances, he clasped his wife in his arms, exclaiming at the same time:

"I am so glad to be back again, as I've lost every

penny in the world, except all the money I settled on you, my darling!"

Then perceiving the company somewhat confused at this unexpected salutation, he thus courteously addressed them: "Pardon me, honoured ladies and gentlemen, but I was not master of my own actions. Mister Barlow, permit me to shake your hand, while I congratulate myself in making the acquaintance of so distinguished a circle, of which you, sir, are the brilliant light, and whom, from what I have heard of you, I have always loved and reverenced. Do not interrupt your festivities on my account. Take my wife as partner for the mazy dance, while I assist your gyrations with a tune upon my faithful banjo." So they set to work to dance in right good earnest; and Harry, later in the evening, while they were at supper, rubbed the floor with lard, so that, when they tried to resume dancing, they fell about the place in all directions, and hurt themselves so severely that there had to be a cessation of dancing for full an hour, after which time, however, it was found that every one preferred sitting round in front of the fire, with the sixth bowl of punch steaming in the centre.

Then followed stories which no one had heard before, and which they would never want to hear again, and forfeits, and pipes and more punch, and songs and——and at six in the morning Mr.

and Mrs. Merton were standing in the snow, thumping a haystack, under the impression that they were knocking at their own front door, Mr. Simmons was asleep under the table, Mrs. Simmons was on a sofa, Farmer Sandford lay on the hearthrug where he had fallen in an attempt to get a light from the fire, in order to see how to wind up his watch with the corkscrew, and Mrs. Sandford was snoring in an arm-chair.

Tommy was fast asleep at the feet of Miss Angelina, who was fondly embracing the banjo, being troubled with nightmare; Harry was lying on the kitchen-dresser, with his head in a soup tureen, which was being submitted to an examination by a commission of black-beetles.

And where were Mr. Barlow and old Mrs. Sandford?

Why, on Boxing Day, which falls on the 26th of December, the marriage bells rang, and old Mrs. Sandford would have become Mrs. Barlow, had not her relations, then and there, removed the infatuated old lady, and locked her up.

Mr. Barlow subsequently discovered her in her retirement, and serenaded her, assisted by a solicitor, who came with a legal instrument, and drew up her will for her one moonlight night, in which, as it subsequently appeared, she left every-

thing she had to that eminent man, Mr. Barlow, and nothing at all to any one of the Sandfords, who, however, by the terms of the document were obliged to bury her at their own expense.

As for Tommy and Harry they remained inseparable, and were promised a week's holiday in London at Mr. Merton's expense.

Honest Farmer Sandford finding that it was unworthy of him to quarrel with Mr. Barlow, now recommended him to all his friends, in the highest terms, as the Instructor of Youth; and as Tommy's father is still a very rich man, Honest Farmer Sandford and Mr. Barlow, by agreeing as to their mutual interests, are doing very well.

* * * * * *

And this, for the present, is all I have to say about the immortal trio, Tommy Merton, Harry Sandford, and their beloved tutor, Mr. Barlow.

Illustrated and other Works

PUBLISHED BY

BRADBURY, AGNEW, & CO.

CHOICE AND POPULAR ILLUSTRATED BOOKS.

CARTOONS FROM "PUNCH." By JOHN TENNIEL. A Selection of some of his best and finest drawings, beautifully printed on thick toned paper, from the original Woodblocks, with a Portrait. Elegantly bound in half morocco, price 50s.
⁎ The Two Series are to be had separately, price 21s. each.

FOREIGN TOUR· OF MESSRS. BROWN, JONES, AND ROBINSON. Sketches of what they Saw and Did in Belgium, Germany, Switzerland, and the Rhine. By RICHARD DOYLE. Handsome volume, demy 4to, price 21s.

MANNERS AND CUSTOMS OF YE ENGLISHE. A Series of Illustrations of English Society, by RICHARD DOYLE. With Extracts from Pip's Diary, by PERCIVAL LEIGH. Quarto, half-bound, price 15s.

A MONTH IN THE MIDLANDS. "A Book for the Shires." A Series of Illustrations by Miss G. BOWERS. Printed on a tint, in handsome oblong folio, with appropriate binding, price 10s. 6d.

BUNYAN'S PILGRIM'S PROGRESS. Illustrated with Forty-four Plates and upwards of Seventy Woodcuts by the late CHARLES H. BENNETT. "A splendid Memorial Edition of the Artist." Quarto. Very handsomely bound in cloth, price 21s.

THE CAUDLE LECTURES. By DOUGLAS JERROLD. A beautiful Quarto Edition, graphically Illustrated by CHARLES KEENE. Bound in a cloth cover designed by JOHN LEIGHTON, F.S.A. Price 10s. 6d.

DOUGLAS JERROLD'S STORY OF A FEATHER. Illustrated with upwards of Seventy highly-finished Woodcuts by GEORGE DU MAURIER. A Companion Volume to "The Caudle Lectures." Uniform size and binding. Price 10s. 6d.

HEARTS OF OAK: Stories of Early English Adventure. Related by W. NOEL SAINSBURY (Editor of the Colonial Calendar of State Papers), With Five toned-paper Illustrations, price 5s.

THE NEW TABLE BOOK. An Album of Pictures for Young and Old. Edited by MARK LEMON. With Coloured Plates and Woodcuts, drawn by FREDERICK ELTZE. Quarto, cloth, extra, price 21s.

MARK LEMON'S FAIRY TALES. Illustrated by RICHARD DOYLE and CHARLES H. BENNETT. "An Illustrated Book for Children of the right sort." In a handsome cover, price 7s. 6d.

TOM MOODY'S TALES. Edited by MARK LEMON, and Illustrated by HABLOT K. BROWNE ("Phiz"). "A capital 'Boy's Book.'" Nicely bound, price 5s.

BRADBURY, AGNEW, & CO., 10, BOUVERIE STREET, E.C.

JOHN LEECH'S ILLUSTRATIONS.

PICTURES OF LIFE AND CHARACTER. Comprising nearly 3000 Sketches from the Collection of "Mr. Punch," &c., drawn by the late JOHN LEECH. In 3 folio volumes, half morocco, price £4 1s.; or in 5 separate volumes, boards, price 12s. each.
The Fifth Volume is sold separately in half morocco, to complete sets, price 18s.

PENCILLINGS FROM PUNCH. A Selection of the late JOHN LEECH's Cartoons from "Punch." With Explanatory Notes by MARK LEMON. In one handsome quarto volume, with a Portrait, half morocco, price 31s. 6d.

FOLLIES OF THE YEAR. A Collection of the Coloured Illustrations in Punch's Pocket Book, drawn from year to year by the late JOHN LEECH. With "Some Notes" to each by SHIRLEY BROOKS. Re-published in a handsome folio volume, half morocco, price 12s.

A LITTLE TOUR IN IRELAND. A Visit to Dublin, Wicklow, Killarney, Galway, Connemara, &c. Written by an Oxonian, and Illustrated by the late JOHN LEECH. Square 8vo, cloth, price 7s. 6d.

THE COMIC HISTORY OF ENGLAND. By the late GILBERT ABBOTT A'BECKETT. Illustrated with Woodcuts and Coloured Etchings by the late JOHN LEECH. Demy 8vo, cloth gilt, price 12s.; half calf extra, price 16s.

THE COMIC HISTORY OF ROME. Uniform with the Comic History of England. By the late G. A. A'BECKETT. Illustrated by the late JOHN LEECH. Demy 8vo, cloth gilt, price 7s. 6d.; half calf extra, price 11s.

YOUNG TROUBLESOME; or, MASTER JACKY'S HOLIDAYS. A Series of Coloured Etchings by the late JOHN LEECH. Oblong folio, price 7s. 6d.

SPORTING WORKS.

MR. SPONGE'S SPORTING TOUR. The First of the Series of Sporting Works written by the late EDWARD SURTEES, Esq. Illustrated with Coloured Etchings and Woodcuts by the late JOHN LEECH. Demy 8vo, cloth, price 14s.

HANDLEY CROSS. By the same Author. Price 18s.

ASK MAMMA! By the same Author. Price 14s.

PLAIN OR RINGLETS? By the same Author. Price 14s.

MR. FACEY ROMFORD'S HOUNDS. By the same Author. Price 14s.

PUNCH'S TWENTY ALMANACKS. The complete Series from 1841 to 1860. Containing Illustrations by the late JOHN LEECH, RICHARD DOYLE, JOHN TENNIEL, CHARLES KEENE, &c. Handsome cloth binding, price 5s. 6d.

BRADBURY, AGNEW, & CO., 10, BOUVERIE STREET, E.C.

"Nothing could be prettier than this diamond edition of the Poet."

Opinion of "THE SUN."
"The paper is toned, the type is exquisitely beautiful, the text is Shakspeare, '*pur et simple*.' It is, besides all these, a very marvel of cheapness, as the result of a happy thought most charmingly realized."

THE
HANDY VOLUME
SHAKSPEARE.

In Bindings suitable for Presents.

BOUND IN GREEN CLOTH, *limp, red edges, in a neat cloth case,* price One Guinea.

IN CRIMSON FRENCH MOROCCO, *gilt edges, in an elegant leather case,* price One Guinea and a Half.

IN THE BEST TURKEY MOROCCO, *limp, gilt edges, in case to match, with Lock,* price Three Pounds Ten Shillings.

IN THE BEST RED RUSSIA, *limp, gilt edges, in case to match, with Lock,* price Three Pounds Ten Shillings.

This choice Miniature Edition of "Shakspeare" is in 13 Volumes, 32mo size, and contains the whole of the Plays, Poems, and a Glossary. The volumes are printed on a slightly toned paper of fine quality, with a new, clear, and readable type, on a page free from Notes—and the Text has been arranged from a close comparison of the most trustworthy editions.

BRADBURY, AGNEW, & CO., 10, BOUVERIE STREET, E.C.

www.ingramcontent.com/pod-product-compliance
Lightning Source LLC
Chambersburg PA
CBHW032112230426
43672CB00009B/1713